AMERICA'S RISING STAR CHEFS PRESENTS

COOKING & ENTERTAINING WITH
AMERICA'S HOTTEST NEW CHEFS

Coffee Pairings and Tips
Decorating Tips

SANTA FE PUBLISHING
SAN FRANCISCO

PHOTOGRAPHER
   WILLIAM McKELLAR

BOOK DESIGNER
   BARBARA DENNEY

WRITER
   ANTHONY
   STEPHEN TIANO

EDITORS
   DENNIS ENGEL and
   PAULA ENGEL (recipes);
   DEBORAH PADDISON

STYLIST
   WILLIAM McKELLAR

EXECUTIVE CHEF
   MARK TIANO

SOUS CHEF
   DOUGLAS
   ROTHENBURGER

TECHNICAL ADVISOR
   CHRIS ISERT

INDEXER
   DENNIS ENGEL

PUBLISHING DIRECTOR
   BRAD STAUFFER

PUBLISHER
   ANTHONY TIANO

Copyright© 1995 by Santa Fe Publishing
582 Market Street
Suite 1300
San Francisco, CA 94104
(415) 403-1330

All rights reserved. No part of this publication may be reproduced, stored in a retrieval system, or transmitted in any form or by any means, electronic, mechanical, photocopying, recording, or otherwise, without the prior written permission of the Publisher. For information write: Santa Fe Publishing.

Photographs, illustrations and text contained in Starbucks Coffee tips on pages 4, 12, 20, 26, 34, 42, 50, 58, 66, 72, 78, 86, 94, 102 and 110 are used by permission of Starbucks Coffee Company. All rights reserved.

ISBN: 0-9641403-1-4
Library of Congress
Catalog Card Number: 95-074975

Manufactured in Hong Kong

Cover:
Rick Tramonto's
Lobster Cocktail
with Roasted Garlic
Mashed Potatoes

ii

CONTENTS

2 Monique Barbeau, Fullers, Seattle
Watermelon Salad with Feta, Sumac and Sage Vinaigrette
Herb-Crusted Prawns with Warm Mushroom and Potato Salad
Salmon Salad with Avocado Vinaigrette and Corn Salsa
Saffron Fish Soup with Garlic Croutons and Rouille
Chocolate Banana Croissant Bread Pudding

A PASSION FOR COFFEE
A "PARADISE FOUND" TABLETOP

10 Thomas Douglas, Dahlia Lounge, Seattle
Flash-Fried Squid with Red Pepper–Almond Aioli and Horseradish Gremolata
Pit-Roasted Salmon with Shiitake Relish, Cornbread Pudding and Fried Basil
Slow-Roasted Duck with Green Olives, Fresh Tomatoes and Celery Root Gratin
Chocolate Waffle with Coffee Ice Cream and Espresso-Caramel Sauce

SIMPLY THE BEST WAY TO BREW COFFEE
A RELAXED LUNCHEON AMONG FRIENDS

18 Michael Chiarello, Tra Vigne, Napa Valley
Spiedini of Mozzarella and Two Tomatoes with Basil Oil
Salmon with Corn Whipped Potatoes and Carrot Nage
Pastina "Risotto" with Roasted Peppers and Broccoli
Pork Tenderloin with Molasses, Bacon and Porcini Vinaigrette
Parfait of "Crazy Raspberries"

CAFÉ SOCIETY
A COLORFUL POOLSIDE OASIS

24 Traci Des Jardins, Rubicon, San Francisco
Artichoke Salad of Summer Tomatoes and Spring Beans
Phyllo Tart of Mushrooms, Potatoes and Spinach with Mushroom Jus
Salmon with Olive Oil Mashed Potatoes and Sauce Niçoise
Pan-Roasted Chicken with Oven-Dried Tomato and Arugula Salad
Warm Financier Cakes with Seasonal Berries

SPICING UP YOUR FAVORITE CUP
OLD WORLD ROMANTIC SETTING

32 Thomas Keller, The French Laundry, Napa Valley
Citrus-Marinated Atlantic Salmon with Potato Blinis and Garden Greens
Pearl Barley "Risotto" with Braised Fennel Bulb
Medallion of Lamb with Green and Black Provençal Olives, Eggplant Caviar and Basil-Infused Extra-Virgin Olive Oil
Oven-Roasted Cornish Hens with Spring Leeks and Red Bliss Potatoes
Warm Bittersweet Chocolate Truffle Cake with Burnt-Sugar Cream

THE ART OF ROASTING
A CASUAL OUTDOOR AFFAIR

40 **Octavio Becerra, Pinot Bistro, Los Angeles**
Warm Crab and Fingerling Potato Salad
    with Horseradish, Crème Fraîche and
    Baby Red Oak Lettuce
Grilled Escolar with Rice Beans,
    Smoked Garlic Cloves, Wild Sage
    and a Purple Mustard Sauce
Braised Lamb Shanks and Portobello
    Mushroom with Slivered Celery Root
    and Roasted Garlic
A Quartet of Beef with Savory Pearl Barley
    and a Riesling Mustard Sauce
Warm Chocolate Tart with Coffee
    Nougatine Sauce

COFFEE IN THE KITCHEN
AN EVENING OF INTRIGUE

48 **Alessandro Stratta, The Phoenician, Scottsdale**
Mesquite-Grilled Tiger Prawns with Pesto,
    Cannellini Beans, Grilled Radicchio,
    Fennel and Confit Tomatoes
Tian of Parmigiano and Grilled Vegetables
    with Tomato Compote, Fresh Buffalo
    Mozzarella and Roasted Eggplant
    with Pesto
Mesquite-Grilled Lamb with Tapénade and
    Grilled Provençal Vegetables
Grilled Squab Breast with Foie Gras and
    Artichokes, Wilted Arugula and
    Sherry Vinegar Bolognese Sauce
Mascarpone-Mint Ice Cream, Fresh Figs
    and Vanilla-Lemon Syrup

THE WORLD'S COFFEE FAMILIES
A PERSONAL TOUCH

56 **John Coletta, Caesars Palace, Las Vegas**
"Risotto" of Carrot-Infused Barley with Lobster
Grilled Farm-Raised Striped Bass in Minestrone
    Broth with Braised Belgian Endive,
    Potato Cake, Soybeans and
    Parmesan Cheese Tuilles
Hot Smoked Veal Soufflé with Merlot Wine
    Glaze, Italian Parsley Juice, Grilled
    Shiitake Mushrooms and Vegetable Slaw
Roast Saddle of Rabbit in Savoy Cabbage,
    Yukon Gold Potato Confit, Balsamic
    Vinegar Glaze, Baby Fennel and Beet
    Juices
Apricots and Ginger Baked in Puff Pastry
    with Almonds

COFFEE BLENDING—A TIMELESS ART
AN OLD WEST PICNIC

64 **Scott Peacock, Horseradish Grill, Atlanta**
Grilled Georgia Mountain Trout with
    Green Onion Sauce
Frogmore Stew with Biscuits
Real Pan-Fried Chicken
Fresh Blackberry Cobbler

**STARBUCKS FOUR FUNDAMENTALS
    OF BREWING**
A SOUTHERN MARKETPLACE TABLE

iv

70 Paul Bartolotta, Spiaggia, Chicago

Tuscan Mussel Soup with White Beans
Guazzetto di Cozze e Cannellini
Wide Ribbon Pasta with Asparagus
and Basil *Tagliatelle con Asparagi*
Sautéed Lamb Chops Glazed in Balsamic
Vinegar *Agnello all'Aceto Balsamico*
Oven-Fresh Red Snapper with Artichokes and
Fresh Oregano
Dentice con Carciofi all'Origano Fresco
Strawberries with Zabaione
Fragole allo Zabaione

**AWAY FROM THE TABLE—
IDEAS FOR SERVING COFFEE
A MIDDLE EASTERN ROMANCE**

76 Rick Tramonto, Brasserie-T, Northfield

Lobster Cocktail with Roasted Garlic
Mashed Potatoes
Grilled Yellowfin Tuna with Pasta and Chinese
Vegetables in Copperwell Sauce
Roasted-Hazelnut-and-Herb-Crusted Lamb
with Five-Grain Risotto
Grilled Beef Tenderloin with Artichoke Frittata,
Curried Fried Potato Sticks and Marrow
Triple Chocolate Espresso Cannoli

**TASTING TERMINOLOGY
A TABLE OF ECLECTIC CRAFTS**

84 Alison Barshak, Striped Bass, Philadelphia

Jumbo Lump Crabmeat with Potato Pancakes,
Mango and Baby Greens
Tandoori Baked Whole Fish
Parmesan-Coated Monkfish
Thai Curried Swordfish
Corn Crème Brûlée
with Blueberry Polenta Cake

**EXPLORING ESPRESSO
A TROPICAL RENDEZVOUS**

92 Paul O'Connell, Providence, Brookline

Bibb and Watercress Salad with Hot Mustard,
Toasted Walnut Bread and
Blue Goat Cheese
Wood-Grilled Double-Cut Pork Chops
with Colcannon-Style Mashed Potatoes
Wood-Grilled Quail with Spiced Cranberry
and Persimmon Glaze and a Pilaf of
Quinoa and Red Lentils
Veal Pastrami
New England Blueberry Cake and Stone-
Ground White Cornmeal Cookie
with Summer Berries and Farm Cream

**COFFEE, WINE AND FOODS
A BOUNTIFUL HARVEST**

100 Matthew Kenney, Matthew's, New York

Ahi Tuna Tartare with Fennel, Caraway Toast
and Green Olive Tapenade
Crispy Red Snapper with Eggplant Agrodolce
Lemon Chicken with Moroccan Olives,
Pine Nuts, Toasted Garlic and Couscous
Coriander-Crusted Venison with
Spice-Glazed Sweet Potato
Cherry Soup with Fromage Blanc

**COFFEE AND TEA
THE NEW YORK SCENE**

108 Douglas Rodriguez, Patria, New York

Lobster Ceviche with Hearts of Palm
Shredded Twice-Cooked Lamb over
Boniato Puree with Black Bean Broth
Chicken Escabeche with Fufu and
Plantain Chips
Puteria de Mariscos
Peach Tres Leches

**STARBUCKS COFFEES SELECTED FOR
AMERICA'S RISING STAR CHEFS
A LATIN FIESTA**

v

ACKNOWLEDGEMENTS

America's Rising Star Chefs production, June 1995. Kitchen cabinetry by Wood-Mode.

For the second season of our television series and cooking and entertaining project, we spent the spring and summer of 1995 searching out Rising Star Chefs and stunning decorating ideas to make this a special reference for your kitchen and dining room. We hope this will be a valuable and informative video and print experience that you will enjoy for years to come.

We had so much help that it is hard to begin with the thanks or the credits, but it comes down to a lot of people who care deeply about what they do and how to attain the highest possible quality. The very best chefs, designers, winemakers and coffee roasters available in the country helped with this project.

We salute the passion of our remarkable 1995 Rising Star Chefs.

The idea was created by Anthony Tiano
    nurtured by Jim Lautz
    with help from Lisa Fuchslin,
    Cara Scheel-O'Connor and
    Sharron Ames

We received support from
    ITT Sheraton Corporation
    Starbucks Coffee Company
    The Brita Products Company

Wood-Mode Fine Custom Cabinetry
GE Profile ™ Appliances
Napa Valley Kitchens
The Phoenician, Scottsdale
The Sheraton Harbor Isle, San Diego
CorningWare/Revere Proline
Sunbeam Household Products
Roscan

Special Thanks to
    The American Society of Interior Designers
        Arizona North Chapter
    Potts by Patt of San Diego

Special thanks to my family, who pitched in with support, cheer and hard work when it was most needed. To Kat, Mark, Barbara, Steve and Kaleigh
    Thanks
    Anthony Tiano

INTRODUCTION

AMERICA IS A LAND OF PASSION! It is hard to imagine any other place with such a mixture of lifestyles, backgrounds and the undeniable passion for creating new combinations of flavors. The arts of cooking and entertaining are flourishing in every corner of our land as more and more people find this an enjoyable way to express themselves and create special events for friends and family.

This book is intended to be in regular use in your home. Each of the 15 chapters contains a full dinner party complete with decorating ideas, food and coffee. The recipes have been selected to give you a taste of our chefs' best work. From a "quick stock," to wood-grilled double pork chop, to fresh blackberry cobbler, you should be able to find just the dish you're looking for…and the creative table setting and decorating ideas to frame it beautifully. Plus, pointers from the experts about serving coffees will make you the consummate host, both for your family and also for those special occasions when you entertain friends.

Our 15 Rising Star Chefs for 1995 hail from every region of the country: New York, Atlanta, Boston, Chicago, Phoenix, Las Vegas, Los Angeles, Philadelphia, San Francisco, Seattle and the Napa Valley in northern California. Their dishes range from traditional French cuisine to Italian, from South American to Southern home cooking. They are nominated by a panel composed of leaders in the restaurant, hotel, wine and food industries, and five were nominees for the James Beard Foundation's Rising Star Chef Award. What they share, regardless of their home base or style of cooking, is a passion for what they do, and a dedication to continual learning and growth. They care deeply about the dining experience in their restaurants and the enjoyment of their customers. Each of these 15 remarkable people has brought several recipes to our television series and to this book.

"It's not just learning a new language—but learning to write poetry in that language," says Octavio Becerra, executive chef and partner of Pinot Bistro in Los Angeles, of studying to be a chef. Becerra and his fellow Rising Star Chefs for 1995 speak of the constant striving and learning that are essential to leadership in any profession. And make no mistake—though some may see it as glamorous, this is a very tough profession indeed. It demands long hours, physical stamina, the ability to constantly innovate in the kitchen, marketing savvy to promote one's food and restaurant, as well as an understanding of the day-to-day needs of operating a small (and sometimes not so small) business.

Also constantly striving for excellence are the talented men and women who helped shape the entertaining and decorating sections of each chapter. They provide easy-to-follow guides to creating exciting and innovative settings that we used to show off our chefs' recipes, and that you can duplicate at home. We are grateful for the help we received from the staff at The Sheraton Harbor Isle in San Diego and from a group of eight members of the Phoenix-based Arizona North chapter of The American Society of Interior Designers.

Good food demands good beverages. We know how important the right wine can be, and more and more we are understanding the variety of good coffee as well. We have included recommendations from our friends at Starbucks Coffee Company on choosing coffees to complement the food.

"You look out on a packed Saturday night and see people eating and socializing; you just stand there and say—Wow—this is unbelievable, this is what I do for a living," says Alison Barshak, executive chef of Striped Bass in Philadelphia. That passion and joy for cooking is the main ingredient in the recipe for creating a Rising Star Chef.

To these men and women and to their cooking styles, add a dash of information about coffee, and wrap it all together with easy-to-follow ideas for setting the stage in your home.

There's only one thing left to say…Enjoy!

MONIQUE BARBEAU

Fullers

Seattle, Washington

"I was always in the kitchen as a kid. I catered all through high school and worked in a fish store," says award-winning executive chef Monique Barbeau of Fullers in Seattle. At 19, this Vancouver, British Columbia native headed east in search of fame. She graduated from the Culinary Institute of America in 1987, and received a bachelor of science degree in hospitality management from Florida International University in Miami in 1991. From there she went on to work in three of New York's four-star restaurants: The Quilted Giraffe, Le Bernardin and Chanterelle. Today, she has found her niche in her own back yard.

Barbeau came to Fullers in 1992 to fill the position of executive chef. Her duties now include responsibility for administration, and financial and staff management. Since her arrival, Fullers has received many awards, including a four-star rating in the *Seattle Best Places Guidebook* and selection by *Pacific Northwest* Magazine as Seattle's best restaurant for two consecutive years. Barbeau was also a co-recipient of the 1994 James Beard Foundation award recognizing the "Best Chef of the Pacific Northwest."

WATERMELON SALAD
with Feta, Sumac and Sage Vinaigrette

HERB-CRUSTED PRAWNS
with Warm Mushroom and Potato Salad

SALMON SALAD
with Avocado Vinaigrette and Corn Salsa

SAFFRON FISH SOUP
with Garlic Croutons and Rouille

CHOCOLATE BANANA CROISSANT BREAD PUDDING

STARBUCKS COLOMBIA NARIÑO SUPREMO COFFEE

appetizer/serves six

Watermelon Salad with Feta, Sumac and Sage Vinaigrette

WATERMELON SALAD
- ¼–½ fresh seedless watermelon, cut into 18 thin triangular slices
- 3 teaspoons sumac (plus some for garnish)
- 4 tablespoons julienned cucumber
- 2 tablespoons finely diced red onion
- 6 tablespoons finely diced feta cheese

Saffron Fish Soup with Garlic Croutons and Rouille *(see page 7)*

AMERICA'S HOTTEST NEW CHEFS

3 teaspoons chiffonade of sage (for garnish)
4 ounces sage vinaigrette (recipe follows)

Dust watermelon slices with sumac.

SAGE VINAIGRETTE

1 bunch fresh sage
1 bunch fresh parsley
1 teaspoon chopped fresh garlic
2 teaspoons chopped fresh shallots
1½ lemons, juiced
1 cup extra-virgin olive oil
salt and freshly ground pepper

Destem sage and parsley and place in a blender. Add garlic, shallots and lemon juice. Pulse to blend. With the motor running, drizzle in oil to create a smooth emulsion. Season with salt and pepper. Put in a squeeze bottle and keep cold until ready to use.

To Serve: In the center of each plate, arrange three pieces of watermelon in overlapping fashion. Combine cucumber, onion and feta with 1 ounce of vinaigrette. Place a small mound of cucumber mixture on each watermelon slice. Top each mound with chiffonade of sage. Using the squeeze bottle, surround watermelon with designs of sage vinaigrette. Dust plate with sumac for garnish.

entrée/*serves six*

Herb-Crusted Prawns with Warm Mushroom and Potato Salad

PRAWNS

12 prawns, shelled and deveined (save shells)
1 egg white, lightly frothed
¼ cup chopped mixed herbs
2 tablespoons olive oil
¼ cup sherry vinegar
1 cup prawn stock (recipe follows)
2 tablespoons butter
juice of ½ lemon
salt and pepper

Lightly coat prawns in egg wash and dredge in herb mix. In a sauté pan, cook prawns in oil over medium heat for 2 minutes. Remove prawns and deglaze pan with sherry vinegar. Reduce until dry, then add prawn stock and bring to a boil. Lower heat and swirl in butter. Season this sauce with salt, pepper and lemon juice.

Dave Olsen, Starbucks Coffee senior vice president, coffee, for *America's Rising Star Chefs*

A Passion for Coffee

"Coffee is not just a beverage, it's a part of life. Coffee should be an experience that you can enjoy and count on every day of your life. There are so many choices now—coffees from different regions of the world, different roasts and blends. There are so many opportunities to learn about coffee, and it's just fascinating.

"Everybody can find a coffee they like. Learn a little bit about coffee so that you can understand better what you enjoyed. Try different things and keep adding to the list of the things you like. Coffee is something to enjoy every day—what you like and what tastes good to you becomes *your* coffee."

4

MONIQUE BARBEAU

Chocolate Banana Croissant Bread Pudding

5

AMERICA'S HOTTEST NEW CHEFS

PRAWN STOCK

- 2 tablespoons olive oil
- ¼ cup diced onion
- 1 diced carrot
- ½ stalk celery, diced
- shells from prawns
- ¼ cup white wine
- 1 tablespoon tomato paste
- 2½ cups water or fish stock
- 1 bay leaf
- 2 sprigs thyme
- 5 peppercorns, crushed

In a saucepan, sauté onion, carrot and celery in oil over medium heat until lightly caramelized. Add prawn shells and stir until shells turn pink. Deglaze with white wine and reduce until dry. Stir in tomato paste. Add liquid (water or stock) and spices. Bring to a boil, then reduce to a simmer for 15 to 20 minutes. Strain liquid, making sure to press down on the solids in order to extract full flavor. Return liquid to pan, and over medium-low heat reduce to a yield of 1½ cups.

MUSHROOM AND POTATO SALAD

- 4 medium Red Bliss potatoes, halved and sliced
- 6 tablespoons olive oil
- 4 cups assorted mushrooms (oyster, cèpe, Portobello, shiitake, chanterelle), sliced
- ¼ cup chopped shallots
- salt and pepper

In a sauté pan, cook potatoes in 2 tablespoons of the oil over medium heat until golden brown and tender. Keep warm. In another sauté pan, cook mushrooms in small batches in oil over medium-high heat until golden brown. Toss in some shallots at the end of each batch and season with salt and pepper. Combine potatoes and mushrooms and keep warm.

To Serve: In the middle of a shallow individual serving bowl, place a generous spoonful of warm mushroom and potato salad. Pour sauce over salad and place two prawns on top.

entrée/*serves six*

Salmon Salad with Avocado Vinaigrette and Corn Salsa

SALMON

- 6 5-ounce salmon fillets
- 2 tablespoons whole cumin
- 1 tablespoon whole coriander
- 1 tablespoon kosher salt
- 1 tablespoon olive oil

Dredge salmon fillets in mixture of spices and salt. In a sauté pan, sauté salmon in oil over medium-high heat until desired doneness.

CORN SALSA

- 3 ears corn
- ½ cup chopped red onion
- 1 jalapeño pepper, finely diced
- 3 tablespoons chopped fresh cilantro
- ¼ cup rice wine vinegar
- 2 tablespoons olive oil
- ½ avocado, diced
- salt and pepper

Lightly cook corn and remove kernels from cob. In a large bowl, gently combine all ingredients except avocado. Cover and refrigerate up to 2 hours. Just before serving, toss in avocado. Serve chilled.

SHALLOT RINGS

- 6 large shallots, thinly sliced and loosened into rings
- flour
- olive oil

Lightly dredge shallot rings in flour. Heat some oil in a shallow saucepan. Fry shallot rings over medium heat until golden brown. Drain on paper towel.

AVOCADO VINAIGRETTE

3 avocados, peeled and quartered
3 limes, juiced
3 tablespoons rice wine vinegar
¾ cup olive oil
salt and pepper

Combine all ingredients except oil in a blender. With the motor running, slowly add oil until well emulsified. Season with salt and pepper. Cover and refrigerate. Vinaigrette may be prepared up to 3 days in advance.

FOR THE SALAD

6 cups mesclun or spring lettuce mix
1 bunch fresh chives, cut into 1-inch pieces

To Serve: Toss mesclun, shallot rings and chives with avocado vinaigrette. Divide among six plates. Top each serving with heaping spoonful of corn salsa and place a piece of salmon on top.

entrée/*serves eight*

Saffron Fish Soup with Garlic Croutons and Rouille

SOUP

2 tablespoons olive oil
½ onion, thinly sliced
1 stalk celery, sliced
1 bulb fennel, sliced
1 large leek, sliced
1 cup white wine
8 cups fish stock
pinch of saffron
6 cloves garlic, sliced
2 cups canned whole tomatoes, finely chopped
bouquet garni (containing 3 parsley stems, celery tops, fennel seed, peppercorns, bay leaf and 1 crushed garlic clove)
2 tablespoons Pernod
salt and pepper

In a saucepan, sauté onion, celery, leek and fennel in oil over medium heat for 3 minutes. Add white wine and reduce by half. Add fish stock, saffron, garlic, tomatoes and bouquet garni. Simmer for 30 to 40 minutes. Remove from heat, squeeze out and discard bouquet garni, and add Pernod. Season with salt and pepper.

ROUILLE

3 red bell peppers, roasted and peeled
1½ cups bread pieces, rough-cut
1 large shallot, roughly chopped
1 clove garlic
2 tablespoons chopped basil
¼-½ cup extra-virgin olive oil
pinch of cayenne pepper
salt and pepper

Moisten bread with water and squeeze out liquid. In a blender, puree bell peppers, bread, shallot, garlic and basil. Slowly drizzle in oil. Season with cayenne, salt and pepper.

GARLIC CROUTONS

8 slices bread, such as peasant bread, cut into 1½-inch circles
1 clove garlic
olive oil

In a sauté pan coated with oil, lightly cook bread rounds until golden brown and crisp. Rub with garlic clove while still warm.

POACHED FISH CUBES

1 cup cubed fish
olive oil
garlic

¼ cup white wine

Sauté fish in olive oil and garlic. Moisten with white wine and keep warm.

GARNISHES

12 black olives, julienned
8 sprigs fennel

To Serve: Pour hot soup into large shallow bowls. Place a heaping spoonful of rouille in middle of bowl. Sprinkle sautéed fish cubes around rouille, and garnish with olives and fennel sprig. Float crouton in soup. Serve immediately.

dessert/*serves eight to ten*

Chocolate Banana Croissant Bread Pudding

PUDDING

2 whole eggs
3 egg yolks
5 tablespoons cocoa
1½ cups brown sugar
1 cup heavy cream
2½ cups milk
pinch of salt
1 vanilla bean, split and scraped (seeds reserved)
½ teaspoon nutmeg
½ teaspoon cinnamon
3 tablespoons sugar
½ cup brandy
4-5 croissants
4 bananas
3 tablespoons butter, plus more for pan
splash of lemon juice
powdered sugar (for garnish)

Preheat oven to 375 degrees. Butter bottom and sides of a 2-quart baking dish. In a bowl, lightly beat together eggs. Add cocoa and sugar. Whisk until incorporated. Put cream and milk with egg mixture in a double boiler over medium heat. Heat until warm. Add salt, spices, sugar and brandy. Continue cooking, stirring constantly, until liquid thickens.

Cut croissants into cubes. Slice bananas and sauté with butter over medium heat until soft. Add lemon juice. Add croissant cubes and bananas to chocolate mixture and stir well. Pour into baking dish and bake in a water bath for approximately 30 minutes. Let cool for 15 minutes.

CRÈME ANGLAISE

1 quart milk
vanilla bean seeds (reserved from preceding recipe)
⅓ cup sugar
16 egg yolks

In a heavy-bottomed pot, scald milk and seeds from vanilla bean. Set aside. In a bowl, combine egg yolks and sugar. Slowly add some of the milk and vanilla mixture to temper eggs. Pour eggs back into pan with milk. Stir continuously over medium heat until mixture thickens. Remove from heat and let cool.

To Serve: Spoon pudding into dessert bowls. Pour crème anglaise over pudding. (Whipped cream or a favorite chocolate sauce can be substituted if desired.) Dust with powdered sugar.

DECORATING

A "Paradise Found" Tabletop

Design:
Nance Capaldo, Allied ASID
Nance Interiors Limited
Arizona

The exotic South Pacific meets the rugged beauty of the Pacific Northwest in this magnificent seafood menu. This hearty feast, laid out upon a blanket of palm leaves, tropical fruit and flowers, features a bounty from chilly coastal waters. Elements of land and sea are combined to create a fanciful setting. Here's what you'll need:

- 2 bunches emerald palm
- Tropical flowers, such as orchids, birds of paradise, protea
- Variety of tropical fruit, such as papaya, mangos, lemons
- Tall, oversized clear glass vase
- Large decorative bowl
- Collection of seashells
- Spanish moss
- Silk cord or tasseled curtain cord
- Sculpture or figurine (optional)

Casually lay palm branches in a fan on your tabletop and secure by placing a unique sculpture on top. If you don't have a sculpture, the weight of a floral arrangement or collection of fruit will also work.

Fill a large bowl with ice to use as a wine cooler; decorate with fresh lemons and seashells. If you are serving shellfish, display clams, mussels or lobster in with the ice.

Arrange a clear vase with vibrant exotic flowers and tie off with a silk cord. For an unusual surprise, fill the inside of the vase with clusters of Spanish moss or a collection of small fruit or seashells.

Scatter some mangos or papaya about the table for color. Cut a few in half to expose their lush interior.

THOMAS DOUGLAS

Dahlia Lounge
Seattle, Washington

"Dahlia Lounge is a sneaky little name," says Thomas Douglas, executive chef and owner of this Seattle restaurant. "Not too many people know the inside story. It was actually named after a meeting place for some friends of mine. They were having an affair and would often meet at a place they called the Dahlia Lounge."

Douglas began his culinary career as a cook at the Hotel Du Pont in Wilmington, Delaware at the age of 18. After moving to Seattle, he went off track for a while, trying his hand at several professions, including house building, wine selling, railroad car repair and the stock market. Luckily for food fans, he chose to go back to the restaurant business.

With its proximity to Asia, Alaska, California and Canada, the northwest United States is a hot spot for Pacific Rim cuisine and its cornucopia of cultures. Starting with the acclaimed Cafe Sport in 1984, Douglas helped define the nuances of the Pacific Rim style. Later, in 1989, he left the comfortable surroundings of Cafe Sport, and with his wife started his own restaurant (and not-so-secret "meeting place") in the heart of downtown Seattle: Dahlia Lounge.

With acclaim and recognition from the *Seattle Times/Post-Intelligencer* as well as *Money* Magazine, *The Los Angeles Times* and *The New York Times*, Dahlia Lounge has become one of Seattle's premier restaurants. In 1994, Douglas was co-recipient of the James Beard Foundation Award recognizing the "Best Chef of the Pacific Northwest."

FLASH-FRIED SQUID
with Red Pepper–Almond Aioli and Horseradish Gremolata

PIT-ROASTED SALMON
with Shiitake Relish, Cornbread Pudding and Fried Basil

SLOW-ROASTED DUCK
with Green Olives, Fresh Tomatoes and Celery Root Gratin

CHOCOLATE WAFFLE
with Coffee Ice Cream and Espresso Caramel Sauce

STARBUCKS CAFFÈ VERONA® (80/20) BLEND COFFEE

appetizer/*serves six to eight*
Flash-Fried Squid with Red Pepper– Almond Aioli and Horseradish Gremolata

SQUID
1½ pounds squid, cleaned and cut into rings (including tentacles)

Slow-Roasted Duck with Green Olives, Fresh Tomatoes and Celery Root Gratin
(see page 14)

AMERICA'S HOTTEST NEW CHEFS

4 cups flour
2 tablespoons paprika
2 teaspoons salt
2 teaspoons pepper
2 teaspoons dried thyme
peanut oil (for deep frying)
lemon wedges (for garnish)

Mix together flour, paprika, salt, pepper and thyme. Heat 3 to 4 inches of oil to 350 degrees in a large pot with fryer basket. Shake off any excess liquid that may have collected around squid. Dredge squid in flour mixture. Fry quickly in batches until golden (1 or 2 minutes). Do not overcrowd or overcook. Drain on paper towels. Salt lightly if desired.

RED PEPPER–ALMOND AIOLI

1 egg yolk
1 red bell pepper, roasted, peeled, seeded and chopped
2 tablespoons tomato paste
4 teaspoons chopped garlic
2 tablespoons lemon juice
2 tablespoons red wine vinegar
1 tablespoon paprika
1 teaspoon cayenne pepper
1 cup olive oil
1 cup slivered almonds, toasted
salt and pepper

Puree all ingredients except oil and almonds in a

Simply the Best Way to Brew Coffee

The coffee press is a stylish-looking coffee pot, and very easy to use. But what we love most about the coffee press, or plunger pot, is its ability to brew an incomparable cup of coffee with just a few elegant movements. In this simple press method, there is no innovative technology, just glass and stainless steel, coffee and water, and about four minutes time.

Brewing in a coffee press closely duplicates the brewing method used by professional coffee tasters. (Using a small tasting glass, coffee buyers steep the grounds in direct contact with water, then allow them to settle before tasting.) Brewing coffee in a press extracts all of the flavorful and aromatic qualities in fine coffee. Keep in mind that this brewing method enhances the inherent flavors in all coffee, so choose a high-quality, fresh coffee to brew with. A lower-quality coffee's inferior taste will come through even more prominently when brewed in a press.

With these four steps, you can savor rich coffee served elegantly:

Into the press, measure 2 tablespoons coarsely ground coffee for each 6 ounces of water.

Add water, just off the boil, into the carafe.

The grounds will froth up and form a "crust." Stir, then cover the carafe with the top of the press, plunger extended upward.

Let stand for 4 minutes (just enough time to serve dessert). Then plunge, pushing the grounds to the bottom of the carafe. Pour and enjoy.

NICK GUNDERSON

food processor. While motor is running, gradually add oil. Add almonds last, pulsing briefly to retain some texture.

HORSERADISH GREMOLATA

- 2 tablespoons chopped parsley
- ½ tablespoon finely minced lemon zest
- 1 tablespoon fresh horseradish, peeled and grated

Combine ingredients.

To Serve: Serve squid hot with red pepper–almond aioli and lemon wedges. Sprinkle horseradish gremolata lightly over and around squid.

entrée/*serves six*

Pit-Roasted Salmon with Shiitake Relish, Cornbread Pudding and Fried Basil

PIT-ROASTED SALMON

- 6 7-ounce salmon fillets
- ½ cup sugar
- ½ cup kosher salt, plus 1 tablespoon
- 2 teaspoons chopped fresh thyme
- ¼ cup paprika
- 1½ tablespoons coarsely ground black pepper
- butter (for pan-searing)
- oil (for frying basil leaves)
- several whole basil leaves (for frying as garnish)
- lemon wedges (for garnish)

Combine sugar, salt, thyme, paprika and pepper. Coat each fillet with 1 or 2 tablespoons of this rub. Smoke salmon in a smoker at 80 degrees for 1 hour. Remove from smoker and refrigerate until ready to prepare for serving.

CORNBREAD PUDDING

- 5 cups cornbread, cut into 1-inch cubes (cornbread recipe follows)
- 1 tablespoon butter, plus more for pan
- 1 medium onion, thinly sliced
- 4½ cups whipping cream
- 8 eggs
- 1½ cups grated dry jack cheese
- 1½ tablespoons chopped herbs
- 2 teaspoons salt
- 1 teaspoon freshly ground pepper

Chocolate Waffle with Coffee Ice Cream and Espresso Caramel Sauce

Preheat oven to 425 degrees. Butter a deep 8-by-12-inch pan and fill with cornbread cubes. Set aside. Heat 1 tablespoon of butter in a heavy sauté pan. Very slowly sauté onion until soft and golden brown (at least 20 minutes). Set aside. Whisk together cream and eggs. Whisk in caramelized onion, grated cheese and herbs. Season with salt and pepper. Pour mixture over cornbread in pan, and stir to combine. Bake 45 minutes until set and golden. Keep warm.

CORNBREAD

4	cups flour
3	cups cornmeal
4	teaspoons baking powder
4	teaspoons salt
2	cups grated pepperjack cheese
8	eggs
4	cups milk
⅔	cup honey
8	ounces butter, melted

This recipe makes more than necessary for cornbread pudding.

Preheat oven to 425 degrees. In a bowl large enough to hold all ingredients, combine flour, cornmeal, baking powder, salt and grated cheese. In another bowl, whisk together eggs, milk and honey. Pour wet ingredients into dry and mix well. Stir in melted butter. Pour into a buttered pan (full "hotel" pan, about 12 by 16 inches) and bake about 25 minutes.

SHIITAKE RELISH

12	ounces shiitake mushroom caps, wiped clean
2	teaspoons pure olive oil, plus some for brushing mushrooms
2	tablespoons finely chopped shallots
2	teaspoons finely chopped garlic
2	tablespoons chopped mixed herbs (e.g., thyme, rosemary, sage, oregano, parsley)
1	tablespoon lemon juice
2	tablespoons balsamic vinegar
¼	cup extra-virgin olive oil

salt and freshly ground pepper

Brush mushroom caps with olive oil. Grill on both sides until marked and cooked through. Remove from grill and julienne. Set aside. Heat pure olive oil in sauté pan. Add shallots and garlic, and sweat a few minutes until soft. Set aside to cool. Combine mushrooms, shallot-garlic mixture and herbs. Whisk together vinegar, lemon juice and extra-virgin olive oil. Pour over mushrooms. Season with salt and pepper.

To Serve: Deep-fry basil leaves in hot oil until crispy. Drain on paper towels. Preheat oven to 450 degrees. In a hot sauté pan with a little butter, sear pit-roasted salmon fillets briefly, nice sides down. Then flip, and sear underside briefly. Place in oven 4 to 5 minutes, or until just done in center. Spoon warm cornbread pudding onto plates. Top with salmon. Spoon some shiitake relish over fish. Sprinkle plate with fried basil leaves and garnish with lemon wedges.

entrée/serves four

Slow-Roasted Duck with Green Olives, Fresh Tomatoes and Celery Root Gratin

DUCK

2	4½-pound ducks
4	sprigs rosemary
1	lemon, quartered
8	cloves garlic, peeled

salt and pepper

sprigs of fresh herbs, such as rosemary or thyme (for garnish)

Preheat oven to 500 degrees. Trim wing tips and neck fat from ducks and clean cavities (wing tips, gizzards and necks can be saved for use in stock; following recipe). Place two lemon quarters, two rosemary sprigs and four garlic cloves in cavity of each duck. Salt and pepper ducks. Place ducks on rack in roasting pan and roast 30 minutes at 500 degrees. Turn heat down to 350 degrees and cook 35 to 45 minutes more. Juices should be pink-gray rather than red, and a meat thermometer stuck in the thigh should read 150 to 160 degrees.

Remove ducks from oven and let rest a half hour or more before carving. When ducks have rested, carve each into two boneless breasts and two leg-thigh portions. This can all be done well ahead if desired. Duck can be refrigerated and reheated before serving.

OLIVE-TOMATO SAUCE

- 1 tablespoon olive oil
- 3 cloves garlic, sliced paper-thin
- 2 cups peeled, seeded and diced fresh tomatoes
- ¼ cup flavorful green olives, such as picholine, pitted and either halved or quartered, depending on size
- ¼ cup balsamic vinegar
- 1 cup reduced duck stock (or duck-enriched chicken stock; see below)
- 8 small sprigs fresh thyme
- 3 tablespoons pine nuts, toasted

salt and pepper

To make duck stock for this recipe, reduce to 1 cup about 4 cups of duck stock, if available. If duck stock is not on hand, a duck-enriched chicken stock will suffice. Brown wing tips and other duck parts saved from ducks for this plate (do not use liver). Cover with chicken stock and simmer for approximately 1 hour. Strain and reduce.

Heat olive oil in a sauté pan. Add garlic slices and cook until lightly golden brown. Be careful not to burn garlic. Add tomatoes, olives and balsamic vinegar. Simmer for a few minutes to reduce vinegar slightly. Add reduced duck stock and thyme sprigs. Simmer to reduce to a slightly thickened consistency. Remove sauce from heat and add pine nuts. Season with freshly ground pepper. Check for salt (but remember that olives are salty, so not much more salt will be needed).

CELERY ROOT GRATIN

- 1½ cups heavy cream, or as needed
- 1 pound russet potatoes, peeled and sliced paper-thin
- 1 tablespoon chopped mixed fresh herbs (e.g., rosemary, thyme, oregano, marjoram, parsley)
- ⅔ cup Parmesan cheese
- 1 pound celery root, peeled and sliced paper-thin

butter (for pan)

salt and freshly ground pepper

Preheat oven to 350 degrees. Butter a wide, shallow baking pan. Drizzle bottom of the pan with a little cream. Arrange a layer of potatoes over cream. Season with salt, pepper and some of the Parmesan and chopped herbs. Drizzle with more cream and arrange a layer of celery root over potatoes. Season with salt, pepper, Parmesan and chopped herbs. Drizzle with cream. Repeat until all vegetables are used. Drizzle cream on top and sprinkle with Parmesan. There will be three or four layers of vegetables, but because they are very thinly sliced, gratin will be wide, flat and thin. Vegetables should be well moistened with cream, but not soupy.

Cover pan with foil and bake 25 minutes. Uncover and increase heat to 425 degrees. Bake another 20 to 25 minutes until bubbling and golden and vegetables are cooked through. Cut into large squares.

To Serve: If reheating duck, heat a large sauté pan and put in duck pieces, skin side down, to crisp the skin. Turn pieces over. Spoon accumulated fat from pan and discard. Put pan of duck pieces into a 450-degree oven to heat for 10 minutes.

Place a large square of warm celery root gratin on each plate. Place one breast portion and one leg-thigh portion of duck over gratin (slice breast if desired). Spoon some sauce over duck and let it run onto plate (but do not cover too much of the duck with sauce or skin will not remain crispy). Garnish with fresh herb sprigs.

dessert/*serves eight to twelve*

Chocolate Waffle with Coffee Ice Cream and Espresso-Caramel Sauce

WAFFLE BATTER

- 2 ounces unsweetened chocolate
- 5 tablespoons butter
- 1½ cups flour
- ½ cup unsweetened Dutch-process cocoa powder
- 1¼ cups sugar
- 1½ teaspoons baking powder
- ½ teaspoon baking soda
- pinch of salt
- 1¼ cups sour cream
- 3 eggs
- 1 teaspoon vanilla
- ¼ cup coffee, freshly brewed, cooled slightly

Melt unsweetened chocolate and butter together in a double boiler. Let cool slightly. Set aside. In a large bowl, combine flour, cocoa, sugar, baking powder, baking soda and salt. In another bowl, combine sour cream, eggs and vanilla. Stir this mixture into dry ingredients. Stir in coffee. Stir in melted chocolate and butter. Cook in waffle iron until done (about 3 minutes). (This recipe makes six whole waffles using a waffle iron that takes a 4-ounce ladle of batter). Waffles can be made ahead and reheated on an oven rack.

COFFEE ICE CREAM

- 2 cups half-and-half
- 2 cups whipping cream
- 1 cup sugar
- ½ cup espresso beans, crushed with a rolling pin
- 8 egg yolks, whisked lightly

In a pot, heat half-and-half, whipping cream, sugar and espresso beans to almost a simmer, whisking occasionally to dissolve sugar. Remove from heat and allow to steep for 45 minutes. Reheat almost to a simmer. Temper egg yolks by whisking a ladle of hot cream mixture into them; then add yolks to hot cream. Stir over medium-high heat until mixture is thick enough to coat a spoon. Immediately strain through a fine chinois to remove crushed espresso beans and any curdled egg. Chill, overnight if possible. Freeze in an ice cream maker. (High-quality commercial ice cream can also be used.)

ESPRESSO-CARAMEL SAUCE

- 2 cups sugar
- 2 cups whipping cream
- 3 tablespoons soft butter
- 4 shots espresso

In a heavy saucepan, dissolve sugar in just enough water to make a slurry. Stir over low heat until all crystals are dissolved. Raise heat and cook without stirring over high heat until sugar caramelizes. Swirl pan occasionally to keep color even. When golden brown, remove from heat and add cream all at once, standing back in case of spatters. Return to low heat and stir with wooden spoon to dissolve sticky caramel in bottom of pan. Remove from heat. Add butter and stir to melt. Add espresso. Keep warm, or gently reheat when ready to serve waffles.

To Serve: Cut waffle into quarters and use two quarters for each serving. Heat waffle. Arrange on a dessert plate with two scoops of coffee ice cream. Drizzle with espresso-caramel sauce. If desired, garnish with a little whipped cream and powdered sugar.

DECORATING

A Relaxed Luncheon Among Friends

Design:
Larry Gaines and Don Patt
Potts by Patt of San Diego

Warm earth tones and accents of copper and coffee beans create a relaxing mood for this casual afternoon luncheon. Guests may linger at the sunny table for hours, sipping aromatic brews reminiscent of their favorite café. Various household items and antiques were gathered to create this rustic setting. Some suggestions:

Textured fabrics such as burlap or canvas can be used as an overlay for your table. Simply cut material into a large square and drape over a tablecloth.

Brass and copper pots or coffee urns serve as beautiful vases for floral arrangements, or as decorative containers to hold coffee beans and condiments.

Colorful glasses can be filled with flowers to complement individual place settings. For a personal touch, tie a strand of ribbon around each arrangement and write your guest's name on the ribbon with a brass or gold metallic marker (available at any craft or art supply store).

Create napkin rings from a variety of materials. Packing twine, eucalyptus or ivy can be wrapped and knotted around a napkin for a rustic touch.

Scatter whole coffee beans about the table to enhance the theme.

An antique coffee grinder or favorite collectible may serve as an unusual conversation piece.

Fold napkins into a fan and set into crystal water goblets. Add a sprig or two of rosemary in with each napkin.

MICHAEL CHIARELLO

Tra Vigne

Napa Valley, California

"I want to take great food off its pedestal and return it to the people," says Michael Chiarello, executive chef and owner of Napa Valley's Tra Vigne Restaurant and Cantinetta, an Italian-style delicatessen and food shop.

Chiarello was born in central California and raised amid Italian tradition, with his mother baking bread in an outdoor clay oven and gathering vegetables from her garden for the evening meal. He graduated from the Culinary Institute of America in 1982. In 1985, while executive chef of Toby's Bar & Grill in Miami, Florida, Chiarello was named Chef of the Year by *Food & Wine* Magazine. In 1986, he moved back to California to fill the executive chef position for the then soon-to-open Tra Vigne, which is Italian for "among the vines."

Chiarello is founder of Consorzio Foods, which produces Italian-inspired ingredients for commercial sale, as well as culinary director of Napa Valley Kitchens. He is also a partner in several other dining ventures: Bumps and Ajax Tavern, both in Aspen, Colorado; Caffé Museo, at the newly opened San Francisco Museum of Modern Art; two Pan-O-Rama bakeries; and the soon-to-open Tomatina, a pizzeria in St. Helena, California.

SPIEDINI OF MOZZARELLA
and Two Tomatoes with Basil Oil

SALMON
with Corn Whipped Potatoes and Carrot Nage

PASTINA "RISOTTO"
with Roasted Peppers and Broccoli

PORK TENDERLOIN
with Molasses, Bacon and Porcini Vinaigrette

PARFAIT OF "CRAZY RASPBERRIES"

STARBUCKS SUMATRA COFFEE

appetizer/*serves four*

Spiedini of Mozzarella and Two Tomatoes with Basil Oil

2	¾-pound balls fresh mozzarella
1	large yellow tomato
1	large vine-ripe red tomato
4	tablespoons extra-virgin olive oil
12	basil leaves, julienned
	salt and pepper
4	8-inch wooden skewers

Cut mozzarella balls and tomatoes in half. Set each half on flat

Parfait of "Crazy Raspberries" *(see page 22)*

AMERICA'S HOTTEST NEW CHEFS

side, square off ends, and cut into two ½-inch-thick slices. Season with salt and pepper to taste. On each skewer, arrange two slices of mozzarella, a slice of red tomato and a slice of yellow tomato, alternating cheese and tomato.

To Serve: Set on a plate and drizzle with olive oil. Sprinkle julienned basil over the dish and serve.

entrée/*serves four*
Salmon with Corn Whipped Potatoes and Carrot Nage

SALMON
4   5-ounce salmon fillets
2   tablespoons olive oil
6   ounces fresh carrot juice
½   cup English peas
1   tablespoon sweet butter (optional)
    salt and pepper

Preheat oven to 350 degrees. Season salmon with salt and pepper. Heat olive oil in a sauté pan. When oil begins to smoke, add salmon and cook until first side is brown (approximately 3 minutes). Turn fish over and cook in oven until done (approximately 6 minutes). Remove salmon from pan and pour off any oil. Let pan cool for about 2 minutes, then pour in carrot juice. Add butter, peas and salt and pepper to taste. Warm lightly.

CORN WHIPPED POTATOES
6   tablespoons butter
1¼ teaspoons minced garlic

Café Society

Whether it's a to-go cup on the way to work or a dreamy afternoon break sipped from fine china, coffee is a part of our culture. As espresso enjoyed with friends, at home or at a trendy coffee outpost, coffee is what you make of it. For without it, our meals, our lives and the lives of centuries of coffee-drinkers before us would be infinitely less satisfying.

"Savored as it is from first sip to last, and reviving as it is to the mind and senses, coffee is a wonderful source of both private pleasure and social stimulation. Today, as they first did more than

700 years ago, coffee houses offer a delightful diversity of experiences. You can chat with friends, join in heated discussions or read in solitude. You can study, sketch or write. You can listen to music or hear poetry recited. You can play cards, checkers, backgammon, chess. As an unsung Viennese wit once put it, a coffee house is 'the ideal place for people who want to be alone but need company for it.'

All the while, whatever you choose to do, you can sip and enjoy one of the world's great pleasures."

—Excerpted from *Starbucks Passion for Coffee*

1 bay leaf
¼ teaspoon saffron, packed
1⅓ cups cream
½ pound fresh corn kernels
1½ pounds potatoes

Mill potatoes or puree in a food processor. Set aside. In a sauté pan, sweat garlic in 3 tablespoons of the butter for 2 minutes, until garlic loses color. Add bay leaf and corn. Sauté for 2 minutes. Add saffron and ⅔ cup of the cream. Simmer for 5 minutes.

Puree half of creamed corn mixture in a blender or food processor for 1 minute. In a separate saucepan, heat the remaining ⅔ cup of cream and add milled potatoes. Mix in remaining creamed corn mixture as well as corn puree. Stir until well incorporated and smooth. Finish off with the remaining 3 tablespoons of butter. (This dish can be made ahead and reheated slowly in a sauté pan for serving.)

To Serve: Spoon corn whipped potatoes into center of each plate. Spread carrot juice around potatoes. Place salmon on top of potatoes and serve.

entrée/serves six

Pastina "Risotto" with Roasted Peppers and Broccoli

1 pound dried pastina (#78 Acini di Pepe)
5 tablespoons pepper-infused olive oil
2 tablespoons chopped garlic
3 cups broccoli florets
2 tablespoons chopped fresh thyme
3 cups chicken stock, canned low-salt chicken broth, or vegetable broth
3 red bell peppers, roasted, peeled, seeded and cut into ½-inch dice
1 cup freshly grated Parmesan cheese
4 tablespoons butter (optional)
salt and freshly ground pepper

Bring a large pot of salted water to a boil. Add pastina and cook until it is slightly undercooked (about 11 minutes). Make sure to stir occasionally during cooking to prevent pasta from sticking to bottom of pot. Drain pasta and run under cold water to stop the cooking. Drain again and reserve.

Heat stock or broth. Heat oil in a saucepan over medium-high heat until hot. Add garlic and cook until light brown, moving pan on and off heat as necessary to regulate temperature. Add broccoli and cook until it

Pork Tenderloin with Molasses, Bacon and Porcini Vinaigrette turns bright green (about 1 minute). Season with salt and pepper. Add thyme, which should make a crackling sound as it hits hot pan. Add stock or broth to broccoli mixture and bring to a boil over high heat. Boil until reduced by half. (Preparation to this point can be done ahead, with reserved pasta and stock being combined at time of serving.)

To Serve: Add peppers and cooked pastina to stock and broccoli, and heat to a boil. Stir in ¾ cup of the Parmesan and season with salt and pepper. Swirl in butter, if desired, for a richer-tasting dish. Pour into a heated serving bowl or individual soup plates and sprinkle with the remaining ¼ cup of cheese.

entrée / *serves four*

Pork Tenderloin with Molasses, Bacon and Porcini Vinaigrette

6	tablespoons porcini mushroom-infused olive oil
2	pounds pork tenderloin
½	pound bacon, cut into ¼-inch dice
1	tablespoon finely chopped garlic
1	teaspoon finely chopped rosemary or ½ teaspoon dried rosemary
⅓	cup balsamic vinegar
2	tablespoons dark molasses
1	tablespoon finely chopped fresh flat-leaf parsley
1	bunch baby spinach, cleaned

salt and freshly ground pepper

Preheat oven to 400 degrees. Heat 3 tablespoons of the porcini oil in a heavy ovengoing pan over medium-high heat until hot. Season pork with salt and pepper and cook in pan for 3 to 5 minutes until brown all over. Put in oven and roast to an internal temperature of 165 degrees (about 15 minutes).

When pork has cooked, transfer it to a platter and keep warm. Pour cooking juices from pan over meat. Return pan to medium heat and add bacon. Cook until crisp. Drain off and discard all but 2 tablespoons of fat from pan. Add garlic and sauté over medium-high heat until light brown. Add rosemary and stir. Remove pan from heat, add vinegar, and stir up all brown bits sticking to bottom of pan. Add molasses and stir well. Then, add spinach and sauté until wilted. Adjust seasoning.

To finish sauce, return pan to heat and stir in juices that have accumulated around the pork. Add parsley and the remaining 3 tablespoons of porcini oil. Keep warm.

To Serve: Slice meat ¼ inch thick and arrange slices on heated plates. Spoon sauce over meat.

dessert / *serves four*

Parfait of "Crazy Raspberries"

2	cups fresh raspberries
½	cup superfine sugar
6	tablespoons Consorzio mango vinegar

pinch of salt
pinch of freshly ground pepper

6	biscotti (your favorite)
8-12	fresh mint leaves

sweetened whipped cream or mascarpone cheese

Combine raspberries, sugar, vinegar, salt and pepper in a non-reactive bowl and let marinate at room temperature for 5 to 10 minutes. Crush biscotti. Layer marinated berries, whipped cream and biscotti in parfait glasses. Pile berries on top. Garnish with a dollop of whipped cream or mascarpone cheese and mint leaves.

DECORATING

A Colorful Poolside Oasis

You can create an inviting poolside affair by transforming an ordinary cabana into an intimate, airy setting using affordable fabrics and a little ingenuity. If you don't own a cabana, rent one from a caterer or party supply business in your area. Or whip one together yourself by using a tree in your yard as support. Here's how:

Drape one end of a colored king-size sheet or gauze netting over a jutting tree branch and secure tightly.

Extend sheet out to create a "roof," and use two long sticks or dowels (found at a hardware store) stuck into the ground to tie off and support the other two ends of the sheet. For a flat-topped awning, use branches of equal height to the "support branch"; for a sloping effect, use supports a few inches shorter than the tree branch. Arrange table and chairs underneath.

Allow the vivid color of the cabana to set the scene for your party—keep surrounding color to a minimum. To outfit your cabana, dress up ordinary lawn chairs with slipcovers, which can be rented from a caterer or party supply store or can be purchased at various housewares stores. You can make slipcovers at home as well, by following a simple pattern found in a fabric store. Choose attractive material that will enhance your color scheme. For further embellishment, tie a colorful sash around the back of the chair and make a bow, allowing the ends to trail to the floor.

Choose a monochromatic scheme for your table linens and place settings, or focus on just a few pure colors for a more tailored look.

A centerpiece of vegetables or fruit complements the outdoor theme and is easier to arrange than flowers.

Bring out items from your home, such as candles, vases or a small table for a homey feel.

Houseplants or hanging ferns set in and around the cabana complete the "oasis" look.

Design:
Jamie Herzlinger, Allied ASID
Herzlinger Interior Design
Arizona

23

TRACI DES JARDINS

**Rubicon
San Francisco,
California**

"My first word was 'eat'," says Traci Des Jardins with a smile. By the time she was four years old, this future chef was rolling tortillas with her grandmother and supervising chocolate chip cookie-making with her cousins. By the age of 17, she knew that she wanted to be a professional cook, and she started in Joachim Splichal's 7th Street Bistro in Los Angeles. Under his mentorship, she grew into a seasoned cook. Her extensive training in France included an apprenticeship at the world-famous Troisgros in Roanne. Returning to a sous-chef position at Montrachet in New York, she met owner Drew Nieporent and started a close working relationship that would one day culminate in the opening of Rubicon.

In 1989, she returned to California to open Patina, in Los Angeles, as chef de cuisine. After two years, she moved north and took behind-the-scenes jobs in San Francisco at Aqua with George Morrone and at Elka with Elka Gilmore (both 1994 Rising Stars).

Des Jardins has bloomed at Rubicon, creating a modern, accessible cuisine firmly grounded in French tradition, and incorporating her passion for fresh flavors and sound combinations of food that honor the integrity of the ingredients. Rubicon's celebrity investors are Robert DeNiro, Francis Ford Coppola and Robin Williams, and it is part of Myriad Restaurant Group, which operates New York's Tribeca Grill, Montrachet and Nobu under managing partner Drew Nieporent.

ARTICHOKE SALAD OF SUMMER TOMATOES
and Spring Beans

PHYLLO TART OF MUSHROOMS, POTATOES AND SPINACH
with Mushroom Jus

SALMON
with Olive Oil Mashed Potatoes and Sauce Niçoise

PAN-ROASTED CHICKEN
with Oven-Dried Tomato and Arugula Salad

WARM FINANCIER CAKES
with Seasonal Berries

STARBUCKS ETHIOPIA SIDAMO COFFEE

appetizer/*serves four to six*

Artichoke Salad of Summer Tomatoes and Spring Beans

1	gallon water
¼	cup flour
¼	cup lemon juice, plus some for rubbing artichokes
2	tablespoons salt

Artichoke Salad of Summer Tomatoes and Spring Beans *(see page 24)*

4-6	large artichokes
2	large beefsteak tomatoes, blanched and peeled
3	large shallots, finely diced
6	tablespoons extra-virgin olive oil
2	tablespoons balsamic vinegar
1	bunch basil, cut into chiffonade
½	pound wax (yellow) beans, cleaned and blanched
½	pound Romano beans, cleaned and blanched
½	pound *haricots verts*, cleaned and blanched
1	tablespoon Dijon mustard
1	pint cherry tomatoes of mixed types, halved
	salt and pepper
	baby greens (for garnish)

In a large pot, bring water to a boil. Make a blanc by stirring in flour, lemon juice and salt until dissolved. Trim artichokes down to bottoms by cutting off stems and snapping off leaves. Remove chokes. Rub cut areas of artichoke bottoms with lemon juice. Add artichokes to blanc and cook until tender.

Slice beefsteak tomatoes into eight to twelve ⅛-inch-thick slices. Cut scraps into julienne and reserve. Marinate tomato slices in 2 tablespoons of the olive oil, 1 tablespoon of the balsamic vinegar, shallots, and half of the basil chiffonade. Season to taste with salt and pepper. Blanch the remaining basil and puree in a blender with 2 tablespoons of olive oil. Reserve cold.

Make a mustard vinaigrette by blending mustard with 2 tablespoons of olive oil and 1 tablespoon of balsamic vinegar. Season to taste with salt and pepper.

Split wax beans lengthwise. Cut Romano beans on the bias into long strips. Toss these beans and *haricots verts* with cherry tomatoes, reserved tomato julienne, pureed basil and Dijon vinaigrette. Season to taste with salt and pepper.

To Serve: Place 2 slices of beefsteak tomato on

Spicing Up Your Favorite Cup

Enhancing the flavor of coffee has long been a coffee-drinkers' fascination. From cardamom pods to eggshells, it seems we love to experiment with the flavor of our favorite brew. While Starbucks focus is always to offer coffees that show their best qualities without artifice or additives, you will find a small selection of flavored syrups at our espresso bars. Noticeably absent, however, are the more exotic essences, replaced instead by flavorings that we feel complement, but do not compete with, the rich taste of great coffee.

Our primary commitment is to provide a spectrum of coffee taste experiences for both the newcomer and the discerning coffee lover. It's pure, unadulterated passion. To add a little spice to your coffee (short of discovering a raspberry- or almond-flavored coffee bean growing in the wild), here are a few delicious ways to flavor your cup.

Syrups—Available in a range of flavors. Use ¼ to ½ ounce to flavor a 12-ounce Caffè Latte or drip coffee.

Cardamom—A traditional coffee flavoring. Seeds or ground spice may be brewed together with your coffee grounds, lending a mellow aroma and warm, lingering taste.

Cinnamon—A popular spice. Mull a pot of coffee with cinnamon sticks after brewing, as adding the spice during brewing makes for an astringent cup.

Cloves, Ginger, Nutmeg, Fennel Seed, Saffron—Historically, these spices have been used to flavor coffee, imparting sweetness and heady aromas.

each plate. Place a few leaves of baby greens around and an artichoke bottom on top. Place spring bean salad on top of artichoke.

entrée/*serves eight*
Phyllo Tart of Mushrooms, Potatoes and Spinach with Mushroom Jus

MUSHROOMS

- 5 pounds assorted mushrooms (domestic, cremini, shiitake, oyster, hedgehog, chanterelle and hen of the woods)
- ½ cup clarified butter (quantity approximate)
- 10 shallots, peeled and diced (reserve scraps for following recipe)
- ¼ bunch thyme, picked and chopped (reserve stems for following recipe)
- ¼ bunch Italian parsley, picked, washed and chopped (reserve stems for following recipe)

Clean and slice mushrooms. Reserve stems for mushroom stock (recipe follows). In clarified butter, sauté each type of mushroom separately to a golden brown. Add some of the shallots toward the end of cooking time for each batch, and cook until soft. Mix mushrooms together and add parsley and thyme.

MUSHROOM *JUS*

- mushroom stems
- shallot scraps
- herb stems
- 2 cups chicken stock
- ¼ bunch Italian parsley, picked, washed and chopped
- 4 tablespoons butter
- salt and pepper

Make a mushroom stock by sautéing mushroom stems, shallot scraps, and herb stems in 2 tablespoons of butter until golden. Add chicken stock, and reduce by half. Reserve.

POTATOES AND SPINACH

- 2 pounds Yukon Gold potatoes, scrubbed clean
- 4 bunches spinach, washed and stems removed

Phyllo Tart of Mushrooms, Potatoes and Spinach with Mushroom *Jus*

27

6 tablespoons butter
salt and pepper

Preheat oven to 350 degrees. Rub potatoes with 4 tablespoons of butter. Salt and pepper. Roast until cooked through. Slice.

Sauté spinach in 2 tablespoons of butter. Season with salt and pepper. Drain well and cool.

TARTS

12 sheets phyllo dough
½ cup clarified butter (quantity approximate)
¼ bunch thyme, picked and chopped
salt and pepper

Preheat oven to 350 degrees. Cut each sheet of phyllo dough into quarters and keep covered with a damp towel. For each tart, remove six quarter sheets of phyllo from protective towel. Brush first sheet with butter and sprinkle with some thyme, salt, and pepper. Repeat to form two stacks of three sheets each. On one stack, place three slices of potato, a little spinach, and one-eighth of the cooked wild mushrooms. Place the second stack of phyllo on top of the first, butter side down. Roll up all edges to seal. Bake for 10 minutes, or until golden brown.

To Serve: Reheat mushroom *jus*. Strain through a fine strainer. To finish sauce, add 2 tablespoons of butter, salt, pepper and parsley. Place a phyllo tart on each plate and drizzle mushroom sauce on top.

entrée/serves four to six

Salmon with Olive Oil Mashed Potatoes and Sauce Niçoise

SALMON

6 5-ounce salmon fillets, skin on

Grill or sear salmon, skin side down, until flesh is medium rare and skin is crisp.

OLIVE OIL MASHED POTATOES

6 russet potatoes
¼ cup extra-virgin olive oil, plus 2 tablespoons
½ bunch Italian parsley, washed and leaves picked
salt and pepper

Cut potatoes into quarters or sixths, depending on size. Bring to a boil in salted water. Cook until tender but not mushy. Drain off water. Mash with ¼ cup of the olive oil using an electric mixer with paddle attachment. Salt and pepper to taste. (Potatoes can be mashed by hand, but that will result in a more textured product.) Drizzle with an additional 2 tablespoons of oil, adjust seasoning, and add Italian parsley.

Olive oil mashed potatoes can be prepared ahead of time to a finished state, then heated in a 400-degree oven for service.

SAUCE NIÇOISE

6 Roma tomatoes, blanched, peeled and seeded
12 fava bean pods, shelled, the beans blanched and peeled
8 cloves garlic, blanched three times and sliced
4 sun-dried tomatoes, chopped
¼ cup Niçoise olives, pitted and roughly chopped
½ bunch scallions, thinly sliced
1 bunch basil, leaves only
extra-virgin olive oil
balsamic vinegar
salt

Dice Roma tomatoes. Start to slowly cook them in scant olive oil, seasoning with salt to release liquid. Add fava beans, garlic, sun-dried tomatoes and olives. Cook until everything is thoroughly hot and flavors are blended.

To Serve: Add basil and scallions to sauce. Also

add a hint of balsamic vinegar to brighten the flavors. Place warm mashed potatoes on a platter or on individual plates. Place salmon on top of potatoes and drizzle sauce around.

entrée/*serves eight*

Pan-Roasted Chicken with Oven-Dried Tomato and Arugula Salad

PAN-ROASTED CHICKEN

- 2 whole breasts from natural chickens, halved
- 4 thighs from natural chickens

Preheat oven to 450 degrees. Place chicken, skin side down, in a very hot sauté pan and roast in oven for 12 to 15 minutes, or until cooked through.

TOMATO AND ARUGULA SALAD

- 3 pounds Roma tomatoes blanched and peeled
- ¾ cup extra-virgin olive oil
- 2 sprigs thyme, stems removed
- 3 tablespoons balsamic vinegar
- 1 bunch basil, cut into chiffonade
- 2 large shallots, diced
- 2 bunches arugula
- salt and pepper

Cut outside "petals" from tomatoes (core and seeds may be saved for tomato sauce). Using ¼ cup of the olive oil, lightly oil a sheet tray and sprinkle with thyme, salt and pepper. Place tomato petals on tray and put in a 200-degree oven for 2 to 3 hours or until lightly dried.

Whisk together balsamic vinegar and the remaining ½ cup of olive oil. Season with salt and pepper. Set aside.

To Serve: Add basil and diced shallot to vinegar and oil when the chicken is cooked. Toss arugula and oven-dried tomatoes with this vinaigrette and place in center of a platter. Place chicken pieces on top.

dessert/*serves eight*

Warm Financier Cakes with Seasonal Berries

FINANCIER CAKES

- 18 ounces ground almonds or almond flour (meal)
- 3½ cups powdered sugar, sifted
- ¾ cup all-purpose flour, plus some for molds
- 5 egg whites
- 1½ cups melted butter, plus some for molds
- ½ teaspoon almond extract

Preheat oven to 400 degrees. Mix almond meal, powdered sugar and flour in a bowl. In another bowl, beat egg whites until stiff. Stir melted butter and almond extract into dry ingredients. Fold in egg whites to complete batter. Butter baking cups or molds and dust with flour. Spread batter into molds evenly and bake for 7 to 10 minutes (longer, if molds are deep), until golden around edges.

BERRIES

- 2 baskets assorted berries, cleaned (slice strawberries)
- 3 tablespoons granulated sugar

Mix sugar and berries and let sit for about 20 minutes.

To Serve: Place a warm financier cake on each plate and serve with berries.

DECORATING

Old World Romantic Setting

Grace your table with the sophistication and Old World elegance of a majestic floral topiary. Fresh white linen and muted pastels complement the softness of the design. A bit of patience is required for assembly, but the result is stunning. Here's what you'll need:

- A 6" to 8" diameter papiér-mâche pot (or any pot to serve as a base)
- 1 to 2 square feet of small-gauge chicken wire
- Plaster of Paris
- Pipe cleaners
- 3 blocks of floral foam (Oasis), pre-soaked in water
- Floral tape or masking tape
- An 11½" diameter designer tray or round pan
- 3 feet of branches, such as curly willow (or any suitable branch)
- Various greens, such as asparagus fern, leather fern
- Variety of flowers, such as Queen Anne's lace, lilies, sweet peas, tulips
- 3 or 4 strands of ivy
- Cinnamon sticks

TO CREATE A BASE FOR THE TOPIARY

First, make sure the height of your topiary will not obscure your guests' vision across the table. After determining the optimum height, cut branches to size. Tie branches into a bundle with pipe cleaners and secure at bottom and center to form a trunk.

Mix plaster of Paris according to directions on box. Position "trunk" of branches in center of pot, and pour plaster to fill pot. Position trunk in pot against a wall or table to keep upright and set to dry. Allow at least 20 minutes drying time.

Once pot is fully dry, place in center of round tray. Cut block of floral foam into pieces and position around bottom of base tray to fill space around the base of the pot. Position additional pieces of foam on top of plaster in the pot around the "trunk." Wrap both top and bottom with tape in a criss-cross pattern to secure foam. The object is to secure the pot of branches to the base tray.

CREATING THE FLORAL TOP

Wrap one block of floral foam with chicken wire (this will keep it from crumbling). Spread apart top of branches and nestle wired foam vertically down into center of branches. Wrap tape outside and around top branches to secure foam in place.

To decorate topiary, position greens in floral foam at very bottom of tray, around the base of the trunk and at the top. Arrange flowers among the greens.

Remove the pipe cleaners from the trunk and finish by wrapping strands of ivy diagonally down along the branches. Add water to foam daily.

Design:
Larry Gaines and Don Patt
Potts by Patt of San Diego

THOMAS KELLER

**The French Laundry
Napa Valley,
California**

"The French Laundry is a very special place to me and to the Napa Valley. I wanted to continue that," says chef Thomas Keller of his latest restaurant. Built in 1900 as an actual French steam laundry, this cobblestone building is firmly rooted in the history of Napa Valley. Today, its picturesque country garden and trellised old-fashioned rose bushes add a backdrop of relaxed style to Keller's contemporary American cuisine with French influences.

Born in Southern California, Keller has been schooled in the fine French culinary tradition. He gained recognition at La Reserve and Restaurant Raphael in New York, and served an *estagiere* (apprenticeship) for a year throughout France in the kitchens of Guy Savoy, Michael Pasquet and Gerard Besson.

In the summer of 1994, The French Laundry opened and was quickly named one of the Best Restaurants of 1994 by *Esquire* Magazine. Keller has received numerous accolades, including being named Best American Chef by *Food & Wine* Magazine, and America's Best Hotel Chef by the James Beard Foundation.

appetizer/*serves four*

Citrus-Marinated Atlantic Salmon with Potato Blinis and Garden Greens

MARINATED SALMON

2	pounds salmon fillet
1½	cups kosher salt
¼	teaspoon freshly ground white pepper
½	cup sugar
1½	teaspoons lemon zest
1½	teaspoons orange zest
1½	teaspoons lime zest
1½	teaspoons grapefruit zest

CITRUS-MARINATED ATLANTIC SALMON
with *Potato Blinis and Garden Greens*

PEARL BARLEY "RISOTTO"
with *Braised Fennel Bulb*

MEDALLION OF LAMB
with *Green and Black Provençal Olives, Eggplant Caviar and Basil-Infused Extra-Virgin Olive Oil*

OVEN-ROASTED CORNISH HENS
with *Spring Leeks and Red Bliss Potatoes*

WARM BITTERSWEET CHOCOLATE TRUFFLE CAKE
with *Burnt-Sugar Cream*

STARBUCKS VIENNESE BLEND COFFEE

Citrus-Marinated Atlantic Salmon with Potato Blinis and Garden Greens *(see page 32)*

The Art of Roasting

It is during the roasting process that the potential of fine coffees is drawn out. Of course, starting with the best coffee is essential. Before Starbucks coffees reach the roaster, the last step on their way to you, we have already done the hard work of selecting exceptional coffees from the world's finest growing regions. But without the artful skill of our roasting experts, all this work would come to naught.

Over the course of only 11 to 15 precious minutes, the beans' temperature rises as high as 450°F. Their color progresses from straw-green to yellow-orange to light cinnamon—then to an optimal rich chestnut-brown. Along the way the beans lose 18 to 25 percent of their weight, while doubling in size. Their progression is marked by a distinct popping sound as oils from the beans begin to seep out.

When these volatile flavor oils develop, the beans' character is fully realized and every flavor element is in perfect balance. It is this quality that we call the Starbucks Roast.® The roaster chooses this precise moment to halt the roasting and release the beans into a rotating cooling tray. A powerful fan draws off their heat. The beans darken one final shade as they swirl around, crackling with heavenly aroma.

Salmon must be prepared at least one day ahead (and may be kept for up to one week). Line a sheet pan with a piece of aluminum foil large enough to envelop the fish. Place half of the salt, pepper and sugar on the foil. Place salmon on salt mixture, skin side down. Rub flesh side with citrus zest and remaining salt, pepper and sugar. Fold aluminum foil over and place another sheet pan, weighted, directly on top of salmon. Place in the refrigerator. (This will help extract liquid as well as compact flesh.) Let marinate for 24 hours. Remove salmon from marinade and rinse under cold water. Pat dry.

POTATO BLINIS

1	pound russet potatoes, peeled
3	tablespoons milk
3	tablespoons flour
3	eggs
3	tablespoons crème fraîche or heavy cream
3	egg whites

salt and freshly ground white pepper

Cook potatoes as for mashed. Pass them through a ricer. Add milk and flour and mix well. Add remaining ingredients, one at a time, whole eggs first, then cream, then egg whites. Mix in each ingredient until thoroughly incorporated before adding the next. Season with salt and white pepper.

To cook, heat a pancake griddle to 325 degrees, spoon blini mixture about a tablespoon at a time onto griddle, and cook as for pancakes. This should be done at the last minute to insure that blinis stay warm.

CITRUS VINAIGRETTE

2	ounces lemon juice
2	ounces lime juice
2	ounces grapefruit juice
2	ounces orange juice
1	ounce white wine vinegar
4	ounces extra-virgin olive oil

Whisk all ingredients together. (This recipe makes more than enough. Store in a container that permits shaking to mix ingredients before using.)

GARDEN GREENS

    1   cup greens, washed and dried

To Serve: Place warm blinis in center of each plate. Top with three slices of marinated salmon. Dress greens with vinaigrette and place on top of salmon. Serve immediately.

entrée/*serves four*
Pearl Barley "Risotto" with Braised Fennel Bulb

BRAISED FENNEL

    4   bulbs fennel, trimmed
    6   quarts boiling salted water
    1   lemon, halved
    2   tablespoons sweet butter
    1   cup chicken stock

Preheat oven to 375 degrees. Place fennel and lemon in boiling water on stove and cover with a towel. Cook until fennel is tender. Remove from water and cool under running water. Cut each bulb into six pieces. In a sauté pan, heat butter and add fennel. Brown on all sides. Add stock and place in oven. Cook for 20 minutes. Remove and reserve twelve pieces for garnish. Chop remaining fennel for addition to the risotto.

PEARL BARLEY "RISOTTO"

    1   tablespoon olive oil
    1   small onion, finely chopped
    2   cups pearl barley
    2   cups chicken stock
    3   cups water, boiling
    2   teaspoons kosher salt
    2   tablespoons sweet butter
    ½   cup grated Parmesan cheese
    ¼   cup whipped cream, unsweetened
    2   fennel bulbs, braised and chopped (from previous recipe)
    2   tablespoons chopped fennel sprigs

Heat olive oil in a medium saucepan. Add onion and cook over moderate heat, stirring until softened (about 3 minutes). Add barley and stir to coat with oil. Pour in stock, reduce heat to moderately low, and cook, stirring occasionally, until absorbed. Add boiling water and salt. Continue cooking until barley is creamy and tender. Add whipped cream, Parmesan cheese, butter, chopped fennel and half of the fennel sprigs (reserve remaining fennel sprigs for garnish).

To Serve: Spoon risotto into each soup plate and garnish with three pieces of braised fennel and some of the remaining fennel sprigs. Serve immediately.

Quick Sauce for Lamb

entrée/*serves six*

Medallion of Lamb with Green and Black Provençal Olives, Eggplant Caviar and Basil-Infused Extra-Virgin Olive Oil

MEDALLION OF LAMB WITH GREEN AND BLACK PROVENÇAL OLIVES

- 3 tablespoons vegetable oil
- 6 5-ounce lamb medallions
- 2 tablespoons sweet butter
- quick lamb sauce (recipe follows)
- ½ cup green olives, chopped
- ½ cup Niçoise olives, chopped
- salt and pepper
- 1 tablespoon chopped Italian parsley (for garnish)

Heat oil in a large sauté pan until hot. Season lamb medallions and add to pan. Cook over high flame until meat has caramelized. Turn over and continue to cook until other side has caramelized. Reduce heat. Add butter and cook for 2 minutes. (Total cooking time for medium-rare is 6 minutes.) Remove meat from pan and keep warm. Drain off excess fat, and deglaze pan with sauce. Add olives, and adjust seasoning.

QUICK SAUCE FOR LAMB

- 1½ pounds lamb bones, broken into approximately 1-inch pieces
- canola oil
- chicken or vegetable stock
- vegetables, finely chopped
- butter or extra-virgin olive oil

Within 30 to 45 minutes, this procedure can yield a sauce with the same intense flavor, same viscosity and same rich color as restaurants produce.

Heat a heavy-bottomed saucepan over medium heat with enough canola oil to coat the bottom. Use a pot large enough for bones to fit comfortably in one layer, with enough space to brown on all sides. Add bones to hot oil and pan-roast until well browned on all sides. Discard any oil that has accumulated in the pan in excess of that amount of oil used at the start. Add to this enough water to cover bones by half. Reduce heat and simmer until all liquid has evaporated. Repeat this step using a natural chicken or vegetable stock.

Once second reduction is complete and bones begin to pan-roast, add other flavoring components desired, such as *mirepoix*, tomatoes or herbs (chop fine for maximum flavor extraction). Continue to pan-roast until vegetables are caramelized. At this point, add three times as much liquid as the volume of bones. The liquid is cook's choice: water, stock and half water, or perhaps a small amount of sauce left from a previous recipe.

Reduce volume by half. Strain twice, once through a coarse strainer and then through a fine-mesh strainer (chinois). Reduce a little more if desired. Finish sauce by adding a little butter or extra-virgin olive oil.

EGGPLANT CAVIAR

- 2 large Italian eggplants
- 1 tablespoon Dijon mustard
- ½ cup extra-virgin olive oil, plus 2 tablespoons
- salt and pepper

Wash eggplants. Puncture skin and rub each eggplant with 1 tablespoon olive oil. Bake in 375-degree oven until tender. Remove from oven, cut open, and scrape out meat. Put meat in a piece of cheesecloth and wring out excess moisture. Then place meat in a food processor. Add mustard. Blend while adding olive oil. Season with salt and pepper.

BASIL-INFUSED EXTRA-VIRGIN OLIVE OIL

- 2 tablespoons kosher salt

3   cups tightly packed basil leaves, washed and stemmed
2   cups extra-virgin olive oil
cheesecloth

Bring a 4- or 5-quart saucepan of water to a full boil. Add kosher salt. Add basil and blanch for 45 seconds. Drain in a basket strainer and cool under running water. Squeeze excess water from basil leaves and place them in blender container with olive oil. Begin blending at low speed to break up leaves. Once basil begins to blend freely, turn to high speed and continue blending for 3 to 4 minutes. Place in a glass storage container and refrigerate overnight in order to create an intensely flavored and richly colored oil.

Secure cheesecloth around the rim of a shallow wide-mouthed container. Pour in oil and allow to strain. This will take up to an hour, depending on temperature of oil. After oil has strained, gently wring cheesecloth for maximum extraction. The remaining basil pulp can be used for pesto, as a marinade for chicken, in sauces, or on pasta. Basil-infused extra-virgin olive oil has a refrigerated shelf life of 3 to 4 weeks.

To Serve: Place 1 tablespoon of eggplant caviar in center of plate. Top with lamb medallion, and spoon olive sauce on top. Garnish with chopped parsley and basil-infused olive oil.

entrée/*serves four*

Oven-Roasted Cornish Hens with Spring Leeks and Red Bliss Potatoes

CORNISH HENS

4   Cornish hens
4   bay leaves
4   cloves garlic, crushed
2   tablespoons extra-virgin olive oil
salt and pepper

Preheat oven to 400 degrees. Rinse Cornish hens inside and out, and pat dry. With the aid of a paring knife, remove each wishbone by lifting skin where breast meets neck and scraping meat away from the wishbone. Run fingers along the bone to loosen and pull away from meat.

Season cavities with salt and pepper. Place one bay leaf and one piece of garlic in each bird and truss. Place birds in roasting pan. Drizzle with olive oil and season with salt and pepper. Roast for about 35 minutes.

RED BLISS POTATOES

16   small to medium Red Bliss potatoes
salt

Place potatoes in cold steamer over medium heat. Season with salt. Cover and steam until tender. Keep warm.

RAMPS

24-28 ramps (young wild leeks; if small market leeks are substituted, reduce the number)

Trim coarse outer leaves and discard. Cut off green tops. Wash white and green parts thoroughly.

Bring a large pan of water to a boil and add salt (it should taste like seawater). Add white portions of ramps or leeks and bring back to a rapid boil. Continue cooking until tender (3 to 4 minutes). Drain and cool quickly under cold running water. Repeat process with green portions, making sure to cook thoroughly, and reserve for sauce.

SAUCE

2   cups chicken stock
4   ounces white mushrooms
½   teaspoon white wine vinegar
cooked ramp tops (from preceding recipe)
salt and pepper

Wash and stem mushrooms. Poach them in chicken stock for 4 to 6 minutes. In a blender, puree all ingredients except salt and pepper. Strain through a fine-mesh strainer (chinois) and adjust seasoning. Adjust consistency, if desired, by adding more chicken stock.

To Serve: Bone Cornish hens. Cut potatoes into quarters, mix with the ramps or leeks, season, and reheat in steamer. Divide the mixture of ramps/leeks and potatoes among four plates. Place hens on top and spoon the sauce around.

dessert/*serves four*

Warm Bittersweet Chocolate Truffle Cake with Burnt-Sugar Cream

CAKE

11	ounces Valrhona Equatorial Chocolate
10	tablespoons butter
6	egg yolks
6	egg whites
4⅔	ounces almond flour (by weight)
1⅔	ounces all-purpose flour (by weight)
7	tablespoons superfine powdered sugar

Chop chocolate and butter into small and equal-sized pieces. Place in a double boiler to melt. Meanwhile, sift all-purpose flour and almond flour. Once chocolate/butter mixture has completely melted, remove from heat. Whip egg yolks with half of the sugar until ribbon stage is reached. Add to chocolate mixture. Begin to whip egg whites with the remaining sugar. Meanwhile, add dry ingredients to mixture and mix well. When whites reach soft-peak stage, fold them into mixture until well incorporated.

GANACHE

18	ounces Valrhona Equatorial Chocolate
2¼	cups heavy cream

Heat cream to a boil. Meanwhile, chop chocolate into small and equal pieces. Pour hot cream over chocolate and mix until chocolate melts thoroughly. Place this ganache in a bowl over an ice bath until firm enough to roll. Roll into logs approximately ¾ inch in diameter and store in freezer until needed.

Brush four molds (2½ inches wide and 1¼ inches deep) with butter and line with parchment paper that reaches ¾ inch above rim. Pipe a small amount of cake mixture into the bottom. Place a ganache plug in the center and cover with more cake mixture. Store in freezer until ready to bake.

BURNT-SUGAR CREAM

1	cup sugar, generously measured
½	cup water
2	cups heavy cream

Place sugar in a saucepan, add water, and heat slowly while stirring with a wooden spoon. Be careful not to splash any sugar onto sides of pan. When liquid starts to form large bubbles, stop stirring. Continue cooking until sugar reaches a rich amber color. Remove from heat and carefully add ¾ cup of the cream. Once cream has been absorbed, place caramel mixture in a storage container and cool. Whip the remaining cream. When it begins to thicken, add caramel mixture and continue whipping until stiff.

To Serve: Preheat oven to 350 degrees. Place cake molds on nonstick sheet pan and bake for approximately 20 minutes. Remove and let rest for 5 minutes. Unmold onto a plate and top with a spoonful of burnt-sugar cream.

DECORATING

A Casual Outdoor Affair

Design:
Larry Gaines and Don Patt
Potts by Patt of San Diego

It is said that everything tastes better outdoors, and the joy of a lazy picnic with good friends is truly one of life's simple pleasures. So pick a sunny afternoon, pack a picnic basket filled with exquisite culinary delights like the ones created by chef Traci Des Jardins, and head off to your favorite hideaway. Here are some tips for making your *al fresco* adventure a memorable one:

Utensils can be used in an inventive way by incorporating them into individual floral arrangements. For each arrangement, begin by packing an attractive glass or mug with floral foam (Oasis) and fill with water. Choose a selection of flowers, or pick some wildflowers nearby and mount them in the Oasis. Tie a few thin strands of ribbon onto a floral pick (available at a florist or craft store) and push in amongst the flowers. Top off by adding utensils to each arrangement.

Use a handsome basket as a centerpiece and fill with bottles of wine, extra glasses and napkins. Throw in some curled ribbon or wrap a few bottles in iridescent cellophane for pizzazz.

Place a natural garland intertwined with various greens, vines and berries around the base of your picnic basket. Add a few loose blossoms or wildflowers if you like.

Fill wine glasses with linen napkins folded into a fan.

Citronella torches or candles placed around the picnic area add romance while deterring insects at the same time.

Remember to place a plastic drop cloth or blanket under your table cloth to keep moisture and dirt out.

OCTAVIO BECERRA

**Pinot Bistro
Los Angeles,
California**

"It's not just learning a new language—but learning to write poetry in that language," says Octavio Becerra, executive chef and partner of Pinot Bistro in Los Angeles, of studying to be a chef. Becerra was planning a career as a commercial photographer when he met chef (and future partner) Joachim Splichal. A decade later, he was nominated for the "Rising Star Chef of the Year" Award by the James Beard Foundation for his cooking at Pinot Bistro.

Prior to the opening of Pinot Bistro, Becerra apprenticed at three Splichal restaurants, including Max Au Triangle in Beverly Hills. Later, he left to study in France and Spain.

When he returned to the United States, he went to work with Splichal, and in 1990, one year after the opening of Patina, Becerra became chef de cuisine. It was during this period that he and Splichal began planning Pinot Bistro, which was voted "Best New Restaurant" by *Esquire* Magazine and "Best Restaurant in the Valley" by *The Los Angeles Times*.

appetizer / *serves four*

Warm Crab and Fingerling Potato Salad with Horseradish, Crème Fraîche and Baby Red Oak Lettuce

FINGERLING POTATO SALAD

- 8 fingerling potatoes, assorted sizes
- 8 Red Bliss potatoes, assorted sizes

Rinse and sort potatoes to uniform sizes—small, medium and large—with smaller potatoes on top. In a large saucepan, cover sorted potatoes with cold water. Bring to a boil and simmer for approximately 35 minutes, or until potatoes are cooked through. Drain potatoes and allow to cool slightly, then slice.

WARM CRAB AND FINGERLING POTATO SALAD
with Horseradish, Crème Fraîche and Baby Red Oak Lettuce

GRILLED ESCOLAR
with Rice Beans, Smoked Garlic Cloves, Wild Sage and a Purple Mustard Sauce

BRAISED LAMB SHANKS AND PORTOBELLO MUSHROOM
with Slivered Celery Root and Roasted Garlic

A QUARTET OF BEEF
with Savory Pearl Barley and a Riesling Mustard Sauce

WARM CHOCOLATE TART
with Coffee Nougatine Sauce

STARBUCKS ITALIAN ROAST COFFEE

**Warm Chocolate Tart
with Coffee Nougatine Sauce**
(see page 46)

America's Hottest New Chefs

CRAB

1 pound Maryland lump crab meat

Pick crab meat clean to make sure no shells remain. Set aside.

CRÈME FRAÎCHE

3 ounces crème fraîche
kosher salt
freshly ground white pepper
cayenne pepper
lemon juice
½ teaspoon prepared horseradish
½ teaspoon finely chopped flat chives
3 tablespoons finely diced shallots
½ teaspoon finely chopped Italian parsley

Season crème fraîche with salt, pepper, cayenne and lemon juice to taste. Add horseradish, flat chives, shallots and parsley. Mix thoroughly, then gently add cleaned crab meat.

GARNISH

12 baby red oak lettuce leaves
½ teaspoon peppercress (a type of watercress)
½ teaspoon onion sprouts
4 garlic blossoms (optional)

Prepare garnish ingredients by picking through the herbs and lettuce, making sure they are crisp and clean.

To Serve: Toss warm potatoes gently but thoroughly with the seasoned crème fraîche, crab meat and peppercress. Place some of the mixture in the center of each 12-inch dinner plate. Lay the baby lettuce leaves around the dish. Garnish with onion sprouts and garlic blossoms.

entrée/serves four

Grilled Escolar with Rice Beans, Smoked Garlic Cloves, Wild Sage and a Purple Mustard Sauce

RICE BEAN RAGOUT

1 fennel bulb
3 ounces water
2 tablespoons finely diced pancetta ham
¼ cup finely diced shallots
6 tablespoons finely diced carrot
1 tablespoon minced roasted garlic

Coffee in the Kitchen

"Food and coffee pairings are really very important. I think that the more you experience great coffees and experiment with them, the more you'll have a sense of which ones go with what kinds of foods. It's really fun. One of the great things about coffee, and something that people

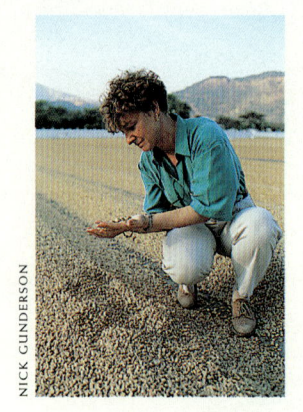

Mary Townsend, Starbucks Coffee vice president, green coffee, for America's Rising Star Chefs

can begin to look at in their kitchens, is how to use different coffees to enhance meals. There's a wonderful world out there, in terms of all the different kinds of coffees that you can taste and prepare at home.

"Use coffee in cooking —if you put espresso in a chocolate dessert, you get a very rich mocha flavor. Coffee makes a wonderful addition to many different kinds of sauces. I use it all the time, and it really gives an interesting, spicy overtone. Coffee is an unusual but readily available spice in your kitchen. I encourage people to experiment with it."

¼	teaspoon wild sage
1	cup rice beans (northern white beans may be substituted)
1½	cups vegetable stock
8	Italian parsley leaves, chopped
6	baby arugula leaves
2	tablespoons extra-virgin olive oil
2	tablespoons purple mustard (Dijon mustard may be substituted)
	kosher salt and freshly ground white pepper
¼	teaspoon bronze fennel (for garnish)

Preheat oven to 350 degrees. Prepare grill. Cut fennel bulb in half and toss with a touch of olive oil. Place halves onto grill and slowly cook until fennel acquires a light smoked flavor and slightly charred look. Transfer to a baking dish. Add water and cover dish with aluminum foil. Slowly bake in oven for approximately 30 minutes, or until tender. Transfer fennel and pan broth to a blender, and puree.

In a saucepan, render the pancetta until golden brown. Add shallots and carrot, minced garlic and wild sage. Sauté for 2 to 4 minutes. Add rice beans, vegetable stock and fennel puree. Bring to a boil, and then simmer for 40 to 60 minutes, or until beans are tender. Strain, and reserve bean broth.

GRILLED ESCOLAR

4	5½-ounce escolar fillets (Pacific sea bass may be substituted)
1	ounce smoked garlic cloves

Preheat oven to 350 degrees. Prepare grill. Grill fish to medium rare. Crush smoked garlic cloves and spread on top of fillets. Place fillets into oven for approximately 3 minutes.

To Serve: Season rice beans with chopped parsley, baby arugula, olive oil and salt and pepper to taste. Place ragout into deep pasta bowls. Finish bean broth sauce by heating it and whisking in purple mustard. Pour sauce around beans. Place garlic-coated grilled escolar onto beans, and garnish with bronze fennel.

entrée/*serves ten*

Braised Lamb Shanks and Portobello Mushroom with Slivered Celery Root and Roasted Garlic

BRAISED LAMB SHANKS

5	1¼-pound lamb shanks
¾	cup peanut oil
1	onion, diced
1	carrot, sliced
½	head celery, sliced (reserve leaves for garnish)
2	heads garlic, separated into cloves and peeled

2	leeks, sliced
1	cup white wine
3	cups lamb or chicken stock
½	bunch parsley, stems only (use leafy tops for celery root recipe)
½	bunch thyme
3	bay leaves
½	pound unsalted butter
10	baby arugula leaves (for garnish)
10	garlic blossoms (for garnish; optional)

Sear lamb shanks in peanut oil. Obtain an even, rich brown color, then remove lamb shanks from pan and set aside.

Add onion, carrot, celery, garlic and leek to pan, and sauté until caramelized to a uniform brown. Deglaze this *mirepoix* with white wine, and reduce until dry. Add stock. Bring to a boil, then simmer. Return lamb shanks to pan, and add parsley stems, thyme and bay leaves. Simmer lamb shanks until tender and beginning to fall off the bone. Lift shanks from braising liquid and allow to cool. Once cooled, remove meat from bones. Strain braising liquid, and reduce until *jus* resembles a sauce that has consistency but is not too thick. Finish with unsalted butter.

PORTOBELLO MUSHROOMS

10	Portobello mushrooms, stemmed
10	cloves garlic, minced
2½	cups chicken stock
1½	tablespoons olive oil, plus some to sauté

Place mushrooms into a casserole or braising dish. Add garlic, stock and olive oil. Bake uncovered in a 325-degree oven until tender (about 30 minutes). Remove mushrooms from braising liquid. Strain liquid, and reduce to a syrup consistency. Reserve.

In a hot sauté pan, sauté Portobellos in a touch of olive oil.

SLIVERED CELERY ROOT

4	celery roots, peeled and thinly sliced
2	onions, peeled and sliced
1¼	cups chicken stock
	pinch of salt
½	bunch parsley sprigs, stems removed (for garnish)

Put celery root and onion into a roasting pan and add chicken stock and salt. Braise until tender. Strain.

ROASTED GARLIC

40	cloves garlic, peeled
	kosher salt and freshly ground pepper
	olive oil

In a sauté pan, toss whole garlic cloves with salt and pepper to taste and enough olive oil to barely cover. Cover with aluminum foil and slowly bake in a 300-degree oven until tender (about 25 minutes). Once tender, strain cloves and reserve the oil.

To Serve: Heat lamb shanks and roasted garlic together in a fair amount of the lamb sauce. Toss celery root with parsley sprigs. Place some celery root mixture onto the center of each dinner plate. Place a Portobello mushroom directly onto the celery root. Carefully spoon braised lamb onto mushroom. Drizzle the plate with a touch of Portobello syrup and olive oil reserved from the roasted garlic. Garnish with fresh celery leaves, arugula and garlic blossoms.

entrée/serves four

A Quartet of Beef with Savory Pearl Barley and a Riesling Mustard Sauce

SWEETBREADS

1	quart water
5	ounces white wine vinegar
6	ounces veal sweetbreads
	butter

Prior to cooking, rinse sweetbreads in cold water for at least 24 hours. Bring the specified water and vinegar to a boil. Briefly blanch sweetbreads in the boiling liquid for approximately 4 to 5 minutes. Strain, and allow to cool. Once cool, peel the thin membrane from sweetbreads. Cut sweetbreads into pieces approximately the size of a marble. Sauté in butter until crispy and golden brown.

OXTAIL AND VEAL

½	tablespoon diced carrot
½	tablespoon diced celery
½	tablespoon diced onion
2	tablespoons minced garlic
2	pieces veal feet
10	ounces oxtail, cut into small pieces
1	quart chicken stock, cold
2	bay leaves
¼	bunch thyme

In a large roasting pan, sauté carrot, celery, onion and garlic. Place oxtail and veal feet in pan, and cover with chicken stock. Bring to a boil. Add bay leaves and thyme. Simmer for 4 to 5 hours. When oxtail is falling off bone, remove from broth and allow to cool. When cooled, separate meat from bones and reserve. Once gelatinous part of veal feet is tender, remove veal from braising broth and allow to cool. Strain broth and reserve. Pick meat from bones and dice into small ¼-by-¼-inch pieces. Reserve.

RIESLING MUSTARD SAUCE

8	shallots, sliced
½	tablespoon butter
½	cup Riesling white wine
2	cups veal braising broth (from preceding recipe)
4	shallots, roasted and sliced
3	sprigs savory, finely chopped
1	tablespoon Dijon mustard

Sauté sliced raw shallots in butter until caramelized. Deglaze with Riesling wine. Reduce by two-thirds, then add veal braising broth. Simmer for 15 minutes. Strain through a fine strainer into a saucepan. Finish sauce with sliced roasted shallots, braised veal feet (from previous recipe), chopped savory and Dijon mustard.

PEARL BARLEY

¼	cup olive oil
¾	cup pearl barley
¼	cup diced celery
¼	cup diced leek
¼	cup diced shallot
2	quarts water
1	smoked ham hock
12	roasted garlic cloves
1	bunch collard greens
1	teaspoon chopped Italian parsley

In a large saucepan, heat olive oil. Add pearl barley and roast slowly for 2 to 3 minutes, stirring continuously. Add celery, leek and shallot. Roast for another 5 minutes, stirring continuously. Add 1 quart of water, and cook slowly until barley is tender. Remove from heat and allow to cool.

Bring 1 quart of water containing smoked ham hock and roasted garlic cloves to a boil. Braise collard greens in this broth until tender. Strain. Chop collard greens into medium pieces.

TENDERLOIN OF BEEF

2	tablespoons peanut oil
4	4-ounce beef tenderloins
	salt and pepper

In a sauté pan, heat peanut oil over a medium-high flame. Season tenderloins with salt and pepper and sauté for 5 to 6 minutes, or until medium rare. Remove from pan and allow to rest.

To Serve: Heat pearl barley with shredded braised oxtail, chopped braised collard greens and chopped parsley. Place in the center of each dish. Slice beef tenderloin and layer over barley. Delicately place sauce around barley and spoon a little over beef. Garnish with crispy sweetbreads.

dessert / *serves fifteen*
Warm Chocolate Tart with Coffee Nougatine Sauce

CHOCOLATE TART

- 6 ounces chocolate, chopped
- ½ cup brewed espresso
- 1¼ cups butter
- ½ cup sugar
- 6 egg yolks
- 6 egg whites
- ½ cup pastry flour

Preheat oven to 350 degrees. Heat coffee and butter, and pour over chocolate. In a bowl, whip ¼ cup of the sugar with egg yolks until firm ribbon forms. In another bowl, whip the other ¼ cup sugar with egg whites to form a light meringue. Combine these three mixtures with pastry flour. Transfer batter to a 9-inch cake pan 2 inches deep. Bake for 15 to 20 minutes, or until tart rises. Remove from oven and allow to cool. Return to oven and bake again until exterior becomes firm but tart is still moist inside.

CRÈME ANGLAISE

- 1 quart milk
- 1 vanilla bean, seeds only (split pod and scrape)
- 1¼ cups sugar
- 16 egg yolks

In a heavy-bottomed pot, scald milk and vanilla bean seeds. Set aside. In a bowl, combine egg yolks and sugar. Slowly add some milk-vanilla mixture to temper eggs. Pour eggs back into pan with milk. Stir continuously over medium heat until mixture thickens. Remove from heat and let cool.

NOUGATINE SAUCE

- 2 cups powdered sugar, plus 5 ounces
- 3 ounces almonds, coarsely ground
- 3½ ounces coffee beans, ground
- crème anglaise (from preceding recipe)

Caramelize sugar in a little water until medium brown. Add almonds and coffee, and stir until smooth. Cook 2 minutes over low heat. Pour out onto a stainless-steel or marble counter (coated with nonstick cooking spray) and spread as smooth and thin as possible. Allow to cool, then break into small pieces. Grind in a food processor until fine. Pass result through a tammy or very fine strainer. Reserve pieces too coarse to go through for use as garnish.

Mix coffee nougatine powder with all of the crème anglaise in a proportion of 3 tablespoons of powder for each cup of crème anglaise. Allow to infuse for at least 1 hour.

KUMQUAT COMPOTE

- ½ cup granulated sugar
- ¼ cup water
- 45 kumquats, cut and seeded
- 15 mint sprigs, julienned

In a heavy saucepan, stir sugar over heat until it dissolves and turns pale brown. Slowly add water. Bring to a boil and simmer for 5 minutes. Place kumquats into this simple sugar syrup. Cool, then add mint.

GARNISH

- ½ pint heavy cream, whipped
- coarse coffee nougatine pieces

To Serve: Heat chocolate tart and place on plates. Pour about 2 tablespoons of sauce on each. Garnish with whipped cream and coarse pieces of coffee nougatine left from the grinding. Spoon sauce around. Garnish with a spoonful of kumquat compote.

An Evening of Intrigue

Design:
Larry Gaines and Don Patt
Potts by Patt of San Diego

Glamour. An ambiance of an era defined by bold strokes of black and white, and streamlined design. The flickering glow cast by tiny oil lamps adds a soft focus to a formal affair. Materials and directions for replicating this opulent oil lamp centerpiece are as follows:

- 4 to 6 clear glass bud vases (varying heights)
- 5 oil lamps filled with oil (available in most gift stores)
- A 6" Plexiglas tray
- Floral foam (Oasis), pre-soaked in water
- Greens, such as maidenhair fern, lemon leaf
- Single flowers, such as calla lilies, orchids
- A 24" to 36" round or square mirror
- 4 to 8 votives
- Glass gemstones

Prepare a base for the oil lamp centerpiece by placing a block of floral foam in the Plexiglas tray. Tape foam in place and arrange greens so that they cover the entire base.

Place mirror in center of table and put tray of greens on top. Next, secure oil lamps of varying height in Oasis filled with greens. (The ones used on this table-setting had long stems, but no bases, thus were ideal for inserting into the floral foam.)

Arrange bud vases on top of mirrored surface with a single flower in each. Place a drop of liquid bleach into each bud vase to keep water clear and fresh. Finally, add a few votive candles at the edge of the mirrored surface and sprinkle gemstones randomly about the arrangement. The candlelight reflecting off the mirror and glass will add sparkle to your table.

DECORATING

47

ALESSANDRO STRATTA

The Phoenician
Scottsdale, Arizona

"I have been fortunate to travel the world, with the opportunity to experience many different cultures, particularly their cuisines and dining traditions," says Alessandro Stratta, executive chef of The Phoenician in Scottsdale, Arizona. "I believe that was an important force in the development of my own style of cuisine, lending an authenticity that is difficult to find in a cookbook."

Stratta follows five generations of his family in the hotel business. He graduated with honors from the California Culinary Academy in San Francisco in 1984. He joined The Phoenician in November, 1989, as chef de cuisine at Mary Elaine's, the resort's formal contemporary dining room. In July of 1993, he assumed the additional responsibility of chef de cuisine of The Terrace Dining Room. Prior to The Phoenician, Stratta held the position of chef saucier under master chef Daniel Boulud at Le Cirque restaurant in New York.

Stratta was nominated in 1992 for "America's Best Chefs—Southwest" by the James Beard Foundation. In 1994, he was named one of "America's Ten Best New Chefs" by *Food & Wine* Magazine. The Phoenician's Mary Elaine's was honored by The Finest Dining Awards (known as the Academy Awards of the Restaurant Industry) with their Gold Award in 1993, and the DiRoNA (Distinguished Restaurants of North America) Mark of Excellence in 1994 and 1995.

appetizer/*serves four*
Mesquite-Grilled Tiger Prawns with Pesto, Cannellini Beans, Grilled Radicchio, Fennel and Confit Tomatoes

CONFIT TOMATOES
- 10 Roma tomatoes, peeled and seeded
- 2 cups extra-virgin olive oil

MESQUITE-GRILLED TIGER PRAWNS
with Pesto, Cannellini Beans, Grilled Radicchio, Fennel and Confit Tomatoes

TIAN OF PARMIGIANO AND GRILLED VEGETABLES
with Tomato Compote, Fresh Buffalo Mozzarella and Roasted Eggplant with Pesto

MESQUITE-GRILLED LAMB
with Tapénade and Grilled Provençal Vegetables

GRILLED SQUAB BREAST
with Foie Gras and Artichokes, Wilted Arugula and Sherry Vinegar Bolognese Sauce

MASCARPONE-MINT ICE CREAM,
Fresh Figs and Vanilla-Lemon Syrup

STARBUCKS KENYA COFFEE

Mesquite-Grilled Lamb with Tapénade and Grilled Provençal Vegetables *(see page 53)*

NICK GUNDERSON

The World's Coffee Families

Many nations within the equatorial coffee belt produce fine *arabica* coffees. While coffees will differ from one country or area to the next, those in each general coffee-growing region in the world exhibit common characteristics that you can learn to recognize, linking them to a geographic coffee "family."

East Africa and Arabia
Beans from the region that gave birth to coffee generally have rich flavor, sparkling acidity, unique floral or winy qualities, and medium to full body. Popular coffees from this family are Ethiopia, Kenya, and Mocha coffees from Yemen.

Indonesia and the Pacific
Dutch traders spread coffee cultivation to Indonesia by the late 17th century. These coffees are usually smooth, earthy and exotic tasting, with low acidity and full body. Enjoy coffees from Java, Sulawesi, Sumatra and New Guinea from this family.

Americas
The French, Dutch and Portuguese began cultivating coffee here in the 1720s. Today's best coffees from this family are clean-tasting and lively, with light to medium body. Included in this group are Colombia, Costa Rica, Guatemala and Panama, as well as coffee from Kona.

2   heads garlic, broken into cloves and left unpeeled
1   bunch thyme
salt and white pepper

Preheat oven to 300 degrees. Place tomatoes in a baking pan with olive oil and salt and pepper to taste. Crush garlic cloves and scatter around tomatoes. Add thyme. Place in oven and bake for approximately 45 minutes, or until the tomatoes have cooked down to a quarter of their size. Cool at room temperature in the oil. Remove from oil and place evenly on another baking pan. (Strain oil and reserve for further use. Save the garlic and thyme to use in stocks.) This recipe makes extra.

GRILLED VEGETABLES AND GREENS
2   fennel bulbs
1   head radicchio
2   cups hearts of romaine lettuce
2   cups arugula leaves
½   cup basil leaves
4   confit tomatoes (see preceding recipe)
4   tablespoons extra-virgin olive oil
1   tablespoon lemon juice
2   cups cannellini beans, cooked with garlic and rosemary
salt and white pepper

Cut fennel bulbs into ¼-inch wedges and cut radicchio into eight wedges. Season with salt and white pepper. Drizzle with a small amount of the olive oil. Grill over mesquite until fennel is golden brown and soft and radicchio is lightly colored and wilted. Chill.

Clean hearts of romaine; use only the small, white middle leaves. Rinse and set aside. Pick leaves of arugula and basil; rinse and drain well. Mix romaine with arugula and basil and warm confit tomatoes. Set aside.

PESTO SAUCE
1   cup chopped fresh basil
2   tablespoons chopped pine nuts

1 tablespoon chopped garlic
2 tablespoons grated Parmesan cheese
½ cup olive oil

Place all ingredients in a blender and puree until well blended.

GRILLED TIGER PRAWNS

16 tiger prawns, shelled
¼ cup pesto sauce (see preceding recipe)
4 8-inch wooden skewers

Place four prawns on each skewer and grill over mesquite. Brush with pesto sauce.

To Serve: Toss greens in olive oil and lemon juice. Season with salt and white pepper. Place a mound in center of each plate. Mix cannellini beans with chilled fennel and radicchio, and place on top of greens. Remove shrimp from grill and lay on top of vegetables. Drizzle with pesto sauce.

Mesquite-Grilled Tiger Prawns with Pesto, Cannellini Beans, Grilled Radicchio, Fennel and Confit Tomatoes

entrée/serves four

Tian of Parmigiano and Grilled Vegetables with Tomato Compote, Fresh Buffalo Mozzarella and Roasted Eggplant with Pesto

TIAN OF PARMIGIANO AND GRILLED VEGETABLES

1 tablespoon diced garlic
2 tablespoons minced shallots
1 tablespoon minced thyme
1 tablespoon balsamic vinegar
1 tablespoon extra-virgin olive oil
1 red bell pepper
1 yellow bell pepper
1 yellow tomato
1 red tomato
1 zucchini
¾ cup Parmesan cheese, grated
salt and cracked white pepper
2 tablespoons tapénade (pureed black olives; for garnish)
2 cups mixed greens (for garnish)

In a bowl, mix garlic, shallots, thyme, vinegar and oil with seasonings. Roast and peel bell peppers.

Cut them with a 1½-inch round cookie cutter and grill. Cut the hearts of tomatoes in the same round and place in garlic mixture. (Reserve tomato scraps for tomato compotes; recipes follow.) Cut zucchini in the same fashion and grill over mesquite until tender. Place grilled vegetables in marinade with tomato. Reserve.

Drop grated Parmesan by tablespoons onto a hot nonstick skillet. When melted and beginning to brown, remove carefully and cool. Make 12 cheese crisps. Reserve.

EGGPLANT AND MOZZARELLA
- 4 ¼-inch-thick slices eggplant
- 4 ¾-inch-thick slices fresh mozzarella
- 1 tablespoon chopped parsley
- 1 tablespoon chopped chives
- salt and pepper

Salt and drain eggplant. Grill eggplant slices over mesquite. Roll slices of mozzarella in herbs, and salt and pepper to taste. Wrap cheese in layer of sliced grilled eggplant. Reserve, chilled, until needed.

YELLOW TOMATO COMPOTE
- 2 cups yellow tomatoes, including reserved scraps
- 1 teaspoon sherry vinegar
- 1 tablespoon extra-virgin olive oil
- salt and white pepper

RED TOMATO COMPOTE
- 2 cups red tomatoes, including reserved scraps
- 1 teaspoon sherry vinegar
- 1 tablespoon extra-virgin olive oil
- salt and white pepper

Puree pulp of each type of tomato separately. Separately, season and cook each, reducing volume by half over low flame. Finish with vinegar and oil. Pass through a chinois.

SHERRY VINAIGRETTE
- ¼ cup sherry vinegar
- ½ cup olive oil
- 1 tablespoon lemon juice

Whisk together liquid ingredients. Reserve.

PESTO SAUCE
- 2 tablespoons garlic puree in oil
- 5 cups basil leaves
- 2 tablespoons pine nuts, toasted
- ¼ cup Parmesan cheese
- 1 cup extra-virgin olive oil
- 2 tablespoons lemon juice
- salt and pepper

In a blender, puree garlic with basil, toasted pine nuts and cheese at slow speed. Add olive oil in a steady stream and emulsify until smooth. Finish with lemon juice, and salt and pepper to taste. Serve at room temperature.

To Serve: Paint plates with compotes, pesto and tapénade. Toss greens in some of the sherry vinaigrette. Layer vegetables with cheese crisps moments before serving. Cheese crisps must remain crispy.

entrée/*serves four*

Mesquite-Grilled Lamb with Tapénade and Grilled Provençal Vegetables

LAMB

1	cup extra-virgin olive oil
½	cup coarsely chopped garlic
4	sprigs rosemary
2	tablespoons cracked black peppercorns
8	baby lamb chops, frenched
8	baby lamb T-bone steaks

Mix olive oil, garlic, rosemary and peppercorns. Place lamb in mixture, cover, and refrigerate overnight.

GRILLED VEGETABLES

1	zucchini
1	Japanese eggplant
1	fennel bulb
1	red onion
1	bunch scallions
1	red bell pepper, roasted and peeled
1	yellow bell pepper, roasted and peeled
16	shiitake mushrooms, stems removed
4	Yukon Gold potatoes, boiled
4	tablespoons extra-virgin olive oil
2	tablespoons fresh thyme
4	cloves garlic, peeled and chopped
	salt and white pepper
4	tablespoons tapénade (pureed black olives; for garnish)

Slice zucchini, eggplant, fennel and onion in ¼-inch-thick slices. Marinate all vegetables in olive oil, thyme and garlic. Season with salt and white pepper. Grill over mesquite until golden brown.

To Serve: Place grilled vegetables on each plate. Top with grilled lamb chops and T-bones. Garnish with tapénade.

entrée/*serves four*

Grilled Squab Breast with Foie Gras and Artichokes, Wilted Arugula and Sherry Vinegar Bolognese Sauce

GRILLED SQUAB

1	tablespoon sage
4	6-ounce squabs, breasts only, bones in (reserve remaining squab parts, including giblets, for sauce; recipe follows)
4	tablespoons extra-virgin olive oil
¼	cup garlic cloves
1	tablespoon minced thyme
2	lemons, quartered

Insert sage under skin of each squab breast. Mix remaining ingredients. Marinate squab breasts in this mixture overnight, covered, in the refrigerator.

BOLOGNESE SAUCE

4	tablespoons extra-virgin olive oil
	bones, heads and legs of squabs, chopped
6	cloves garlic, unpeeled
½	cup chopped onions
¼	cup chopped carrots
2	tablespoons butter
4	cups white chicken stock
4	squab livers
4	squab hearts

1 tablespoon sherry vinegar
 2 tablespoons minced parsley
 1 tablespoon minced chives
 1 tablespoon minced basil
 1 tablespoon minced chervil
 salt and pepper

Heat 2 tablespoons of the olive oil in a thick, heavy saucepan until it reaches point of smoking. Add chopped squab bones, heads and legs, and roast until dark golden brown and evenly colored. Add garlic, onions and carrots, and sweat until translucent. Add butter and caramelize. Deglaze with 1 cup of the chicken stock and reduce by half. Add the remaining 3 cups of stock. Simmer for 2 hours at low temperature. Strain stock (squab *jus*) and continue to cook until it reaches sauce consistency.

Place squab livers and hearts in a blender and puree. Heat another saucepan with the remaining 2 tablespoons of olive oil and add liver-and-heart puree. Heat, then deglaze with most of the sherry vinegar and reduce. Add squab *jus*, parsley, chives, basil, chervil and a few drops of sherry vinegar. Season with salt and pepper, and reserve.

GARNISH
 8 artichoke hearts, raw
 2 cups arugula
 ½ cup garlic focaccia croutons
 1 cup shelled and peeled fava beans
 4 4-ounce medallions of foie gras
 sherry vinaigrette (see previous recipe under Tian of Parmigiano and Grilled Vegetables)
 lemon juice

Slice artichoke hearts very thinly with a meat slicer. Reserve in lemon water.

To Serve: Drain sliced artichoke hearts and mix with leaves of arugula, focaccia croutons and fava beans. Toss with sherry vinaigrette. Grill marinated squab breasts to medium rare. Place a bed of arugula and artichoke hearts on each plate. Top with squab breast and a medallion of foie gras. Spoon sauce around.

dessert/*serves four*
Mascarpone-Mint Ice Cream, Fresh Figs and Vanilla-Lemon Syrup

(This recipe comes from pastry chef Richard Ruskell.)

MASCARPONE-MINT ICE CREAM
 1¾ cups sugar
 3 cups water
 17½ ounces mascarpone cheese
 3 tablespoons lemon juice
 15 chopped fresh mint leaves

Bring sugar and water to boil. Remove from heat and add remaining ingredients. Infuse overnight, then strain. Freeze in an ice-cream maker.

VANILLA-LEMON SYRUP
 1 cup sugar
 1 cup water
 2 vanilla beans, scraped (reserve seeds for another use)
 lemon juice

Bring sugar, water and vanilla beans to a boil. Remove from heat and strain. Add lemon juice to taste.

GARNISH
 4 grapefruit sections
 4 figs, halved

To Serve: Scoop ice cream into bowls. Add a grapefruit section and two fig pieces to each. Drizzle with syrup. Serve immediately.

DECORATING

A Personal Touch

Design:
Thomas Cooke
The Phoenician
Scottsdale, Arizona

That rule that says everything has to match…break it! Have some fun! Next time you entertain, let your personality shine through with an eclectic setting, such as this Mediterranean Grill. The key here is simplicity—variety brings out the innate beauty of the natural surroundings and promotes a feeling of looseness and freedom.

These guidelines will help get you started:

Don't hide or cover up natural beauty; if you have a lovely wooden table, for example, don't disguise it by throwing a cloth over it. Keep items simple and unadorned.

Use a collection of cherished items that you may have acquired in your travels or on a recent shopping trip. Place a sundial or small wooden carvings or sculpture next to place settings, for example.

Create objects of interest from natural materials, such as a handmade container adorned with pussy willow branches to hold breadsticks. Here's how to make your own: Cut pussy willow branches (or any type of branch) to size to fit the container you have chosen. Wrap double-sided tape around the circumference of container and affix the sticks. Finish off with a strand of raffia or twine.

Terra cotta flower pot liners function as artsy salad dishes. Further the theme by using a terra cotta or clay planter as a wine cooler.

Keep flower arrangements from looking too "fussy" and over-arranged—a bunch of long-stemmed tulips placed in an antique watering can are highlighted here. (Put a penny or two in the bottom of a vase containing tulips to keep stems from drooping. The copper also oxidizes the water and keeps it from getting stagnant.)

Fill silver or pewter bowls with condiments or black or green olives for style.

Remember, everything doesn't have to be a matched set; an eclectic array is a fantastic look.

JOHN COLETTA

Caesars Palace Hotel

Las Vegas, Nevada

"Whether you spend a week in Napa Valley or work with one of the great master chefs, there has to be a continual education process," says Manhattan-born John Coletta, executive chef at Caesars Palace Hotel/Casino in Las Vegas. Coletta believes a chef's training never ends.

His own background attests to that. He grew up working in his parents' restaurant and received an associate degree in hotel and restaurant management from New York City Community College. Later, he studied at the Culinary Institute of America.

Prior to joining Ceasars Palace, Coletta worked on the teams that opened the Fairmont Hotel-Chicago and the Sheraton Chicago Hotel and Towers, serving as executive chef for both. He has trained with such notable chefs as Pierre Wynants, Pierre Romeyer of Belgium and French master chef Alain Chapel. He was a member of the 1992 gold-medal-winning team representing the United States at the Culinary Olympics in Frankfurt, Germany; he also won an individual gold medal in the 1984 Culinary Olympics.

"I enjoy cooking," he says. "My family was in the restaurant business, going back many generations. Being here at Caesars is kind of a culmination of my dreams of being the best and working with the best."

"RISOTTO" OF CARROT-INFUSED BARLEY
with Lobster

GRILLED FARM-RAISED STRIPED BASS
in Minestrone Broth with Braised Belgian Endive, Potato Cake, Soybeans and Parmesan Cheese Tuilles

HOT SMOKED VEAL SOUFFLÉ
with Merlot Wine Glaze, Italian Parsley Juice, Grilled Shiitake Mushrooms and Vegetable Slaw

ROAST SADDLE OF RABBIT
in Savoy Cabbage, Yukon Gold Potato Confit, Balsamic Vinegar Glaze, Baby Fennel and Beet Juices

APRICOTS AND GINGER BAKED IN PUFF PASTRY
with Almonds

STARBUCKS NEW GUINEA PEABERRY COFFEE

appetizer/*serves six*

"Risotto" of Carrot-Infused Barley with Lobster

"RISOTTO" OF CARROT-INFUSED BARLEY

2	tablespoons extra-virgin olive oil
2	tablespoons finely diced carrot
2	tablespoons finely diced celery
2	tablespoons finely diced leek
2	tablespoons finely diced onion
1	clove garlic confit, minced
9	ounces barley, parcooked
4	cups fresh carrot juice

Grilled Farm-Raised Striped Bass in Minestrone Broth with Braised Belgian Endive, Potato Cake, Soybeans and Parmesan Cheese Tuilles
(see page 58)

2	cups	clear chicken broth
2	cups	clear fish broth
1	ounce	mascarpone cheese
¼	cup	whipping cream
2	tablespoons	freshly grated aged Parmesan cheese

sea salt and freshly ground white pepper

Heat olive oil slowly in a heavy-bottomed pot. Add carrot, celery, leek and onion, and stir slowly using a wooden spoon. Add garlic and barley and continue to stir. In a separate pan, combine carrot juice, chicken broth and fish broth and bring to a boil. Over a medium flame, add half this liquid in stages to barley, stirring and thoroughly incorporating each addition (this should take about 30 minutes). Season barley with salt and pepper to taste. Fold in mascarpone, cream and Parmesan. Reduce remaining carrot and broth mixture by one-third and keep warm.

LOBSTER

3   1-pound fresh Maine lobsters, cleaned

Steam lobsters for 10 to 12 minutes. Remove shells. Cut tail and claw meat into medallions (scraps may be used for some other recipe). Keep warm.

DEEP-FRIED ZUCCHINI FLOWERS

6   zucchini flowers
¼   cup rice flour
2   tablespoons water

Using a paring knife, open zucchini flowers. Combine rice flour and water, and brush mixture onto flowers. Deep-fry at 350 degrees until crisp. Keep warm.

GARNISH

⅔   cup tiny carrot pearls, blanched and lightly sautéed (use a melon baller to cut pearls)
6   Parmesan cheese curls, made from a block of Parmesan cheese
3   chervil sprigs
1   tablespoon olive oil

To Serve: On each warm dinner plate, arrange barley "risotto" and lobster. Garnish with deep-fried zucchini flower, carrot pearls, reduced carrot glaze, Parmesan cheese curls and chervil sprigs. Drizzle with olive oil. Serve at once.

entrée/*serves six*

Grilled Farm-Raised Striped Bass in Minestrone Broth with Braised Belgian Endive, Potato Cake, Soybeans and Parmesan Cheese Tuilles

STRIPED BASS

6   4-ounce farm-raised striped bass fillets, carefully scaled but skin on

Coffee Blending— A Timeless Art

From the first time inventive coffee-traders combined Yemen Mocha and Java coffees to create the incomparable Mocha Java, the world's first coffee blend, blending has been an important part of coffee culture. At Starbucks, our blends are artistic tributes to the quality and selection of our coffees and to our coffee buyers, who expertly map out the flavor profiles for our blends.

Blending coffees parallels the creation of recipes for fine foods. The Starbucks approach to blending is founded on achieving a truly unique taste in the cup. A Starbucks blend fills a taste niche and offers a flavor experience that a single varietal coffee cannot. Simply, coffee blending is the process of combining varietal coffees to achieve balance and distinction. Enjoy a Starbucks signature blend, or experiment on your own with these suggestions: 75% Sulawesi with 25% Italian Roast—elegant and sweet; for home espresso, 80% Espresso Roast with 20% Arabian Mocha Sanani—sweet and mysterious.

olive oil
salt and pepper

Drizzle boned fillets thoroughly with olive oil and season. Refrigerate.

MINESTRONE BROTH

2	tablespoons extra-virgin olive oil
1	1-by-1-inch prosciutto cube
2	tablespoons finely diced leek
2	tablespoons finely diced celery
2	tablespoons finely diced zucchini
2	tablespoons finely diced yellow squash
2	tablespoons finely diced savoy cabbage
2	tablespoons finely diced, peeled and seeded tomato
2	tablespoons finely diced Yukon Gold potato
2	tablespoons finely diced onion
2	tablespoons fresh cranberry beans, shelled
1	clove garlic, minced
1	teaspoon chopped Italian parsley
1	teaspoon chopped sage
1	teaspoon chopped basil
3	cups clear fish broth

sea salt and ground white pepper
nutmeg

Sauté olive oil and prosciutto lightly in a heavy-bottomed pot. Slowly add leek, celery, zucchini, yellow squash, savoy cabbage, tomato, potato and onion, and simmer slowly. Add remaining ingredients, including salt, pepper and nutmeg to taste, and cook slowly over a low flame for 2 hours. Begin to serve when minestrone is ready, first removing prosciutto.

BRAISED BELGIAN ENDIVE

2	tablespoons extra-virgin olive oil
6	medium Belgian endives, quartered lengthwise
1	bay leaf
1	thyme sprig
¾	cup clear chicken broth
1½	tablespoons chicken glaze

sea salt and freshly ground white pepper

Heat a heavy-bottomed skillet. Add olive oil. Brown Belgian endive well on all sides. Add bay leaf, thyme, chicken broth and chicken glaze, and season to taste with salt and white pepper. Simmer over low heat until very tender. Reserve.

POTATO CAKE

1	tablespoon extra-virgin olive oil, plus more for sautéing potato cakes
1	dried fennel stick
1	bay leaf
2	sun-dried tomatoes
3	medium Yukon Gold potatoes
1	teaspoon minced Italian parsley leaves, no stems
1	teaspoon chopped lemon segments
1	tablespoon potato starch

sea salt and freshly ground white pepper

Add 1 tablespoon of olive oil to a heavy-bot-

"Risotto" of Carrot-Infused Barley with Lobster

tomed pot. Quickly sauté fennel stick, bay leaf and sun-dried tomatoes. Add potatoes. Cover with water and cook over a medium flame until potatoes can be cut smoothly with a paring knife. Let cooked potatoes cool to room temperature, then remove skins and rice. Combine with Italian parsley and chopped lemon and season to taste. Form potato mixture into small cakes and dust with potato starch. In a heavy-bottomed sauté pan, sauté potato cakes on both sides in olive oil until golden brown. Remove and keep warm.

SOYBEANS
½ cup fresh soybeans, removed from shell

Heat soybeans and keep warm.

PARMESAN CHEESE TUILLES
3 ounces Parmesan cheese, finely grated

For each of the six tuilles, melt ½ ounce of cheese in a nonstick skillet over a low flame. Carefully remove melted cheese and shape over side of a wine bottle. Tuilles will become crisp as they cool. Reserve.

To Serve: Carefully grill striped bass, making sure skin is not torn. Place potato cake in center of a hot dinner plate. Arrange Belgian endive. Sprinkle soybeans around and ladle on some minestrone. Place bass skin side up. Top with Parmesan cheese tuille. Serve at once.

entrée / *serves six*

Hot Smoked Veal Soufflé with Merlot Wine Glaze, Italian Parsley Juice, Grilled Shiitake Mushrooms and Vegetable Slaw

VEAL SOUFFLÉ
6 veal loin tenderloins
1 egg
1 ounce crushed ice
3 tablespoons spinach puree
2 tablespoons canola oil
1 fresh truffle, cut into 18 thin slices
6 ounces caul fat
4 ounces Merlot vine trimmings or any wood chips of your choice
sea salt and freshly ground white pepper

Trim veal tenderloins by removing all fat, sinew and side strap. Reserve trimmings. Cut each trimmed tenderloin into three 1-inch nuggets. Clean reserved trimmings and free from any fat, sinew or gristle. Grind twice and place in a chilled food processing bowl. Add egg, ice, spinach puree and salt and pepper to taste. Process to mousse consistency. Remove from bowl and refrigerate for 1 hour.

In a heavy-bottomed skillet, sear veal nuggets on both sides in canola oil over a high flame. Remove nuggets from skillet. Using a pallet knife, spread veal-spinach mousse onto nuggets, top each with one slice of truffle, and wrap in caul fat. Place veal soufflés in stovetop smoker that contains ignited vine trimmings or preferred wood chips. Cover and smoke for 20 minutes.

MERLOT WINE GLAZE
3 cups Merlot red wine
1 bay leaf
2 fresh thyme sprigs
1 clove garlic
6 tablespoons chicken glaze

In a heavy-bottomed pot, combine Merlot wine, bay leaf, thyme and garlic. Reduce by 75 percent and then add chicken glaze. Strain and keep warm.

PARSLEY JUICE
2 cups Italian parsley leaves, no stems
1 tablespoon lemon juice
1 clove garlic confit
½ cup clear chicken broth

¼ cup extra-virgin olive oil

Blanch Italian parsley. Combine with lemon juice, garlic, chicken broth and olive oil in a blender for 2 minutes. Remove from blender and reserve.

GRILLED SHIITAKE MUSHROOMS

    18   fresh medium shiitake mushrooms, stems removed
    1   tablespoon minced shallots
    4   fresh thyme sprigs
    4   tablespoons extra-virgin olive oil
         sea salt and freshly ground white pepper

In a bowl, combine shiitake mushrooms, shallots, thyme, olive oil and salt and pepper to taste. Let marinate for 5 minutes. Grill when ready to serve.

VEGETABLE SLAW

    2   tablespoons finely julienned carrot
    2   tablespoons finely julienned red bell pepper
    2   tablespoons finely julienned yellow bell pepper
    2   tablespoons finely julienned green bell pepper
    2   tablespoons finely julienned napa cabbage
    2   tablespoons finely julienned red cabbage
    2   tablespoons finely julienned snow peas
    2   tablespoons finely julienned leek
    2   tablespoons finely julienned fennel
    1   tablespoon chiffonade of basil
    1   tablespoon bean sprouts, cleaned
    1   tablespoon lemon juice
    ¼   ounce walnuts, chopped
    ⅛   ounce white sesame seeds
    ⅛   ounce black sesame seeds
    1   tablespoon balsamic vinegar
    4   tablespoons walnut oil
         sea salt and freshly ground white pepper

In a bowl, combine all and adjust seasoning.

GARNISH

    6   fennel sprigs, deep fried

To Serve: On each hot dinner plate, arrange three veal soufflés and drizzle with Merlot wine glaze and parsley juice. Place grilled shiitake mushrooms around. Center vegetable slaw. Garnish with a deep-fried fennel sprig. Serve at once.

entrée/*serves six*

Roast Saddle of Rabbit in Savoy Cabbage, Yukon Gold Potato Confit, Balsamic Vinegar Glaze, Baby Fennel and Beet Juices

ROAST SADDLE OF RABBIT IN SAVOY CABBAGE

    2   pounds boneless loin of rabbit and tenderloin, free of sinew and silver membrane
    2   tablespoons extra-virgin olive oil
    1   teaspoon chopped basil
    1   teaspoon chopped thyme
    1   teaspoon fresh juniper berries
    6   tablespoons Dijon mustard
    1   egg yolk
    8   heads savoy cabbage, leaves only, blanched
         sea salt and freshly ground white pepper

Preheat oven to 350 degrees. Season rabbit with thyme, basil and salt and ground white pepper to taste. In a heavy-bottomed skillet, heat olive oil over a high flame. Pan-sear rabbit, making sure that meat remains raw inside. Add juniper berries while cooking. Remove rabbit from skillet. Combine mustard with egg yolk and brush on rabbit.

Place blanched cabbage leaves between sheets

of plastic wrap and carefully flatten with a rolling pin. Place rabbit on cabbage and roll up securely, discarding plastic wrap. Place in a roasting pan and roast for 20 minutes. Keep warm.

POTATO CONFIT

12	medium Yukon Gold potatoes
¾	cup duck fat
1	clove garlic
1	bay leaf
1	thyme sprig
¾	cup chicken glaze (for service)
1	cup chive sticks (for garnish)

In a heavy-bottomed pot, combine potatoes, duck fat, garlic, bay leaf and thyme sprig. Simmer very slowly until potatoes are cooked. Remove potatoes from pot, slice, and grill. Reserve.

BALSAMIC VINEGAR GLAZE

1¼	cups balsamic vinegar
1	bay leaf
1	thyme sprig
1	clove garlic
6	tablespoons chicken glaze

In a heavy-bottomed pot, combine balsamic vinegar, bay leaf, thyme sprig and garlic clove. Reduce by 75 percent. Add chicken glaze. Reserve.

BABY FENNEL

2	tablespoons extra-virgin olive oil
12	baby fennel bulbs, trimmed
2	cups chicken broth

Heat olive oil slowly in a heavy-bottomed pot. Add fennel and sauté slowly. Gradually add chicken broth until fennel is tender. Keep warm.

BEET JUICES

6	tablespoons julienned fresh beets
1	tablespoon lemon juice
¾	cup chicken broth

In a heavy-bottomed pot, combine beets, lemon juice and chicken broth and cook over a low flame. Simmer for a moment, then liquify in a blender. Reserve.

To Serve: Using an electric knife, slice the rabbit. Brush grilled potatoes with chicken glaze, sprinkle with chive sticks and arrange in center of a hot dinner plate. Carefully place rabbit slices into potatoes. Place baby fennel in center and carefully drizzle balsamic vinegar glaze and beet juices. Serve at once.

dessert / *serves six*

Apricots and Ginger Baked in Puff Pastry with Almonds

2¼	cups water
1	cup sugar, plus 2 tablespoons
1	vanilla bean, cut lengthwise
1	teaspoon finely julienned ginger
12	apricots, cut into sixths
4	egg whites
4	ounces 10X sugar (superfine powdered sugar)
6	5-inch puff pastry rounds, unbaked
½	cup sliced almonds
¼	cup crystal sugar
	10X sugar in a shaker

In a heavy-bottomed pot, bring water and sugar to a boil. Add vanilla bean, ginger and apricots and let cool to room temperature. Remove vanilla bean. Distribute mixture into individual 8-ounce ramekins.

Preheat oven to 350 degrees. In a stainless-steel bowl, whip 10X sugar into egg whites to form an icing. Wrap tops of ramekins with puff pastry. Drizzle on icing, then sprinkle sliced almonds and crystal sugar. Bake until pastry forms dome.

To Serve: Dust pastry dome with 10X sugar. Place ramekin with a napkin on a base plate. Decorate plate with seasonal flowers. Serve at once.

DECORATING

An Old West Picnic

Design:
Luis Corona, Allied ASID
Casa del Encanto
Phoenix, Arizona

Reinvent images of the Old West by combining readily available ingredients and Western-style plants and accessories for this rustic outdoor dinner party. Pull out the picnic table and even bring it inside to make your guests feel that they are dining out under the stars of the wide-open Western skies. The cacti used in these miniature gardens require little care and will provide long-lasting pleasure. Only a few materials are needed:

- Random collection of stone and clay containers
- 4 containers with 10 to 12 potted cacti per container
- Sand
- River rocks or small stones
- Moss

Plant cacti directly into containers using sandy soil, placing the tallest plants to the rear and scaling them down towards the front. (Be sure to use care in planting, using tongs or gardener's gloves to avoid needles.)

Fill in with dry sandy soil, leaving enough space to place the river rocks around the top.

Arrange the individual cactus gardens around tabletop, set out dinnerware, then top table off with bright napkins. For added interest, an assortment of colorful bandannas can be used as napkins.

Prop with some Old West relics such as a spur or some turquoise stones to add flair.

Be creative and find new uses for old items; a rain barrel, wooden spool table or stack of crates may provide additional buffet space.

SCOTT PEACOCK

Horseradish Grill
Atlanta, Georgia

"Good Southern food is of the highest possible integrity. It doesn't have to be a carbon copy of the past, but it must be prepared with respect," says Scott Peacock, executive chef of the Horseradish Grill in Atlanta.

Peacock recalls shelling peas and pecans as a child growing up in rural Hartford, Alabama, where his mother had a garden and a cow. "I wasn't happy to be doing that until 10 o'clock on a summer night," says Peacock, "but I grew up knowing what real butter and real milk taste like."

At age 24, Peacock was hired as chef to then-Georgia Governor Joe Frank Harris, and became a student of Southern cooking maven Madeleine Kamman and a protegé and culinary soul mate of Edna Lewis, whose home-style recipes brought Southern food to the culinary forefront. In keeping with his heritage, Peacock has joined with Lewis and a group of eminent Southern cooks and authors to form the Society for the Revival and Preservation of Southern Food. "He has revived, and in most cases refined, the glories of Southern cooking," says John Mariani of *Esquire* Magazine, one of our nominating panel members.

entrée/serves six

Grilled Georgia Mountain Trout with Green Onion Sauce

TROUT

- 6   12-ounce freshwater trout, cleaned, with heads and tails left intact
- 6   slices top-quality hickory-smoked bacon, preferably country style
- 6   tablespoons rendered bacon fat (warmed to liquify)
- 12   fresh basil leaves

sea salt and freshly ground pepper

GRILLED GEORGIA MOUNTAIN TROUT
with Green Onion Sauce

FROGMORE STEW
with Biscuits

REAL PAN-FRIED CHICKEN

FRESH BLACKBERRY COBBLER

STARBUCKS HOUSE BLEND COFFEE

Frogmore Stew with Biscuits *(see page 66)*

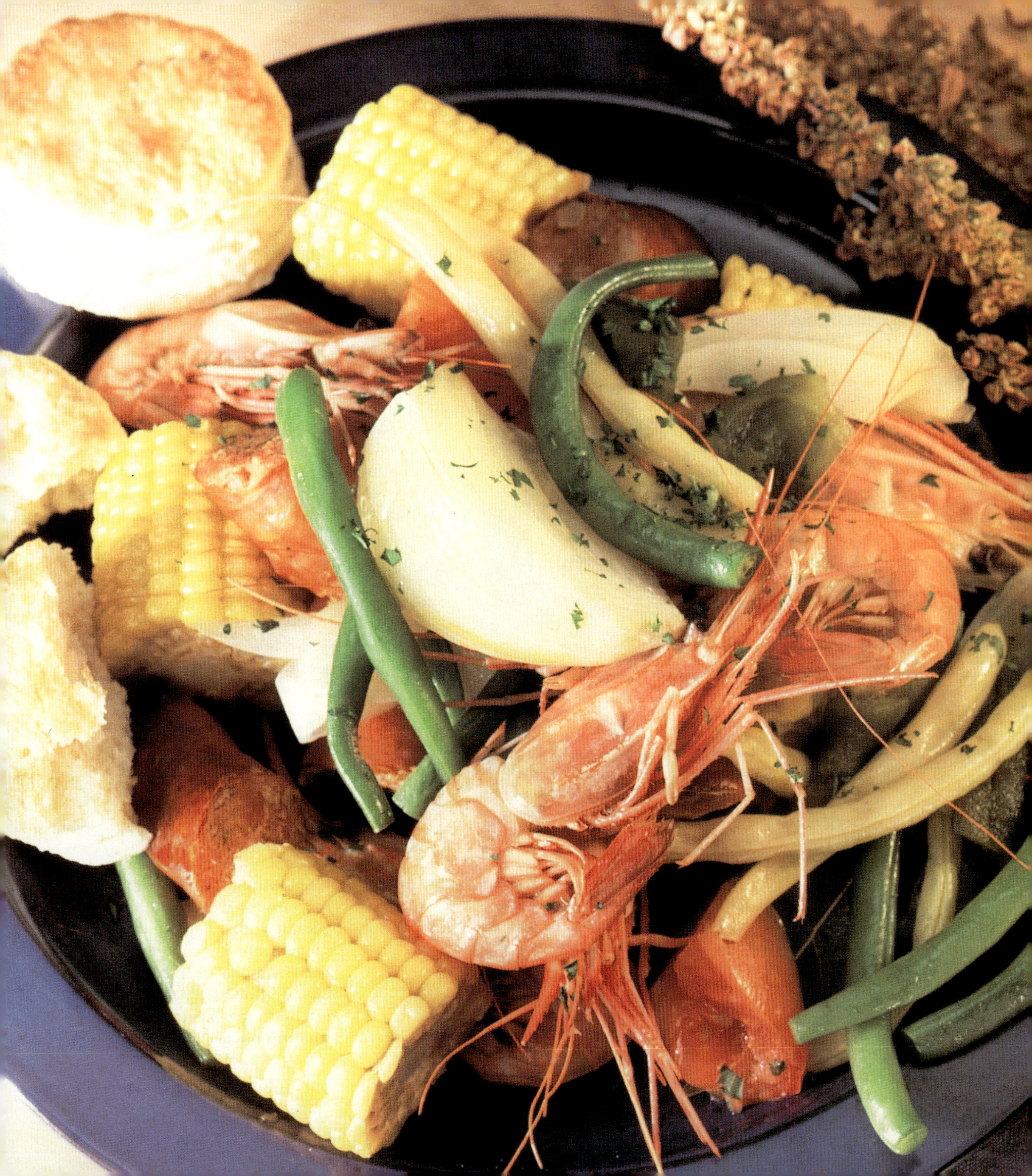

Preheat broiler or start grill. Gently wash trout in cool running tap water. Dry with paper towels. Lightly brush insides of fish with bacon fat. Sprinkle with salt and pepper. Lay two basil leaves in cavity of each trout. Lightly brush outsides of fish with bacon fat. (At least half of bacon fat should be left over.) Sprinkle with salt and pepper. Wrap each trout in a slice of bacon and secure with a toothpick. Refrigerate until ready to cook.

Starbucks Four Fundamentals of Brewing

To enjoy a great cup of coffee worthy of a fine dinner or simply as a relaxing break during the day, we suggest following these simple guidelines.

Proportion
The recipe for coffee using any brewing method: 2 tablespoons coffee grounds for each 6 ounces water. Check your brewer's capacity using a measuring cup, as the marks on the carafe may not always represent a 6-ounce serving.

Grind
Use the proper grind for your brewing method. If your brew is bitter, your coffee may be too finely ground. If your cup tastes weak, your coffee may be too coarsely ground.

Water
Fresh, cold water, heated to just off boiling, extracts the optimum flavor of your coffee. If you don't like the taste of your tap water, try brewing with filtered or spring water instead.

Freshness
Always brew with fresh beans. For the best cup, brew your coffee fresh each time you serve it. Coffee kept over a burner for more than 20 minutes loses its delicious taste.

NICK GUNDERSON

GREEN ONION SAUCE
- 2 egg yolks
- 1 teaspoon sea salt
- 1 tablespoon cider vinegar
- 1 tablespoon freshly squeezed lemon juice
- 1 teaspoon Coleman's dry mustard
- 1½ cups peanut oil
- ½ cup thinly sliced green onions

Combine egg yolks, salt, vinegar, lemon juice and dry mustard in a large ceramic bowl and whisk vigorously until thoroughly mixed. While whisking, slowly add peanut oil in a thin stream in order to fully incorporate into mixture. (Be careful not to add oil too fast or whisk too slowly. Either can cause sauce to break up.) Stir in onions and season to taste. If sauce is too thick, thin with 1 or 2 tablespoons of water.

To Serve: Just before cooking, brush trout with remaining bacon fat. Broil or grill over medium-hot coals approximately 4 minutes, then gently turn and cook other side. Test one fish for doneness after 7 to 8 minutes of cooking. Do not overcook. When fish are done, top with green onion sauce and serve.

entrée/serves six

Frogmore Stew with Biscuits

FROGMORE STEW
- 12 baby red potatoes
- 1½ quarts chicken stock
- 1 large onion, peeled and sliced lengthwise into ⅓-inch slices (leave root intact to hold slices together)
- 1 bay leaf
- 3 sprigs thyme
- 1 pound andouille sausage, cut on the bias into 1-inch pieces
- 3 ears fresh corn, ends trimmed, each cut into 4 pieces

2	medium green bell peppers, roasted, peeled and cut into 1-inch pieces
24	large fresh Gulf shrimp, heads on
1	large tomato, peeled and chopped
1/3	pound green beans, blanched (optional)
1/3	pound wax beans, blanched (optional)
	salt and pepper
	fresh parsley, chopped (for garnish)

Boil potatoes until tender. Keep warm.

Bring stock to a boil. Add onion, bay leaf and thyme, and simmer, partially covered, until almost tender (about 7 minutes). Add sausage and cook for 7 minutes longer. Add corn and roasted peppers. Cook until just tender (about 10 minutes). Season with salt and pepper (the stew should be full-flavored and rich). Bring to a boil, and add shrimp and tomato. Add green and wax beans if desired. Cover and cook for 2 minutes. Do not overcook shrimp.

BISCUITS

2	pounds all-purpose flour
3	tablespoons salt
1/2	cup baking powder, plus 1 tablespoon
1/2	pound lard
4	cups buttermilk
	unsalted butter

Preheat oven to 450 degrees. Sift dry ingredients together in large mixing bowl. Work in lard by hand. Add buttermilk. Blend together well.

Turn onto floured work area. Roll dough out to 1/2-inch thickness. Using a fork, prick dough all over. Cut out biscuits with a biscuit cutter, making sure to cut straight up and down. Do not twist cutter.

Line baking sheet with parchment paper and place biscuits 1/2 inch apart on pan. Bake for 11 to 12 minutes. Remove from oven and brush tops of biscuits twice with melted unsalted butter. (This recipe makes 2 to 2 1/2 dozen biscuits.)

To Serve: Place four shrimp, two pieces of corn, three slices of sausage and some of the peppers, onions and beans from the stew in individual bowls. Cut potatoes in halves. Place four halves in each bowl. Ladle in 1/2 cup of broth and sprinkle with chopped parsley. Serve with biscuits.

Fresh Blackberry Cobbler

entrée/*serves six*

Real Pan-Fried Chicken

PAN-FRIED CHICKEN

1	whole chicken, cut into 8 pieces for frying
2	quarts water, tap or bottled
4 1/2	tablespoons sea salt
1	quart buttermilk
2	cups all-purpose flour
1/2	cup cornstarch
1/4	cup potato flour
1/2	teaspoon freshly ground black pepper

Preparation of this recipe may most conveniently be started the day before serving.

Combine water, 3 tablespoons of salt and chicken in a bowl and refrigerate 8 hours or overnight. Remove chicken from water brine and cover with buttermilk (preferably from whole milk). Combine with 1 tablespoon of salt. Let chicken rest in buttermilk for at least 2 hours or overnight. Remove chicken from buttermilk mixture. With hands, squeeze or wipe off any remaining buttermilk. This will leave a light coating.

Mix all-purpose flour, cornstarch, potato flour, 1½ teaspoons of salt, and pepper. Very lightly dredge chicken in mixture. Take care to cover thoroughly, but shake well to remove excess.

Heat special fat (recipe follows) to 350 degrees in an iron skillet or frying pan. Fry chicken pieces, skin side down first, approximately 5 to 6 minutes on each side, until golden brown and done throughout. Take care not to crowd pieces in pan.

SPECIAL CHICKEN-FRYING FAT

- 1½ pounds fresh high-quality lard
- ½ pound unsalted butter
- 2 thick slices cured pork shoulder or country ham

In a large pot, combine lard, butter and ham slices. Melt fats and cook over medium heat. Skim and clarify as for butter. Cool, strain, and use for frying chicken.

dessert/*serves eight to ten*
Fresh Blackberry Cobbler

PASTRY

- 3 cups unbleached all-purpose flour, sifted
- 1¾ teaspoons salt
- 1 teaspoon granulated sugar
- ½ pound frozen unsalted butter, cut into ½-inch pieces
- 2 tablespoons frozen lard, cut into thin slices
- 8-12 tablespoons ice water
- 5 sugar cubes, crushed

In a large mixing bowl, combine flour, salt and granulated sugar. Cut in butter and lard pieces with pastry blender until mixture resembles very coarse meal; do not overmix. Form a well in middle of mixture and begin incorporating water, 1 tablespoon at a time, until mixture just begins to cling. Mixture should hold together but should not feel damp. Divide dough in half. Wrap each half in waxed paper and refrigerate at least 1 hour before rolling out.

On a cold floured surface, roll out half the dough and line a 2-inch-deep, 2-quart oval baking dish. Cover dish and any excess dough with waxed paper and refrigerate.

FILLING

- 8 cups fresh blackberries, tops removed
- 1 cup granulated sugar
- 1 tablespoon cornstarch
- pinch of salt
- ½ teaspoon freshly grated nutmeg
- 4½ tablespoons unsalted butter, sliced thin

When ready to assemble cobbler, preheat oven to 425 degrees. Remove remaining dough from refrigerator and roll out top crust to fit dish.

Fill pastry-lined dish with berries. In a small bowl, mix together sugar, cornstarch and salt. Sprinkle over berries. Top with nutmeg and 3 tablespoons of butter. Cut any leftover pastry into 2-inch pieces and mix into berries.

Moisten rim of dough in baking dish. Fit top pastry over dish and seal edges of dough together inside dish rim. Cut a few slits in center to allow steam to escape. Sprinkle crushed sugar cubes on top of pastry. Dot with remaining butter slices.

Place dish on baking sheet in preheated oven for 20 minutes. Reduce heat to 375 degrees and bake for 30 to 40 minutes more, or until crust is a deep golden brown.

To Serve: Remove cobbler from oven and cool on a rack. Serve warm.

DECORATING

A Southern Marketplace Table

Design:
Larry Gaines and Don Patt
Potts by Patt of San Diego

The lively bustle of an outdoor marketplace is the inspiration for this hearty Southern meal. Hand-crafted baskets brimming with bursts of vibrant flowers, herb garlands, and terra cotta votives create a festive ambiance that can be easily achieved with a few simple materials.

PLATE GARLANDS
- Wire
- Raffia (straw or twine)
- Rosemary branches
- Various greens, such as eucalyptus or ivy

Begin by cutting a piece of wire about 2" longer than the circumference of your plate. Wind rosemary branches and greens loosely into wire to create a long strip. For added garnish, twist a strand or two of raffia or twine over the herbs.

To finish, wrap the wired greens into a wreath and fasten at ends. Set garlands at each place setting and position plates over each. Remaining herbs or raffia may serve as napkin rings.

MINIATURE FLOWER POT VOTIVES

Enchanting votives made from miniature flower pots further lighten the mood and can be found at any garden center. Here's what you'll need:
- Small terra cotta flower pots (various sizes if desired)
- Sand
- Votive candles
- Raffia or straw

Simply fill pots with sand to prevent candles from tipping and place votives securely in center. If desired, tie each pot with a string of raffia for a more polished look.

PAUL BARTOLOTTA

Spiaggia

Chicago, Illinois

"Two chefs can be equals technically, but the food of the one who has his heart in his work will taste better," says Paul Bartolotta, executive chef of Spiaggia in Chicago. It is this belief that drove the Milwaukee-born Bartolotta, a graduate of the Milwaukee Area Technical College's Restaurant & Hotel Management Program, to spend seven years in Italy, studying and training with his Italian colleagues and ultimately working in some of that country's most prestigious restaurants. While in Italy, he learned the subtleties of *alta cucina* (the cooking of the aristocracy) from Valentino Marcattilii, founding chef of San Domenico in Imola.

Under Bartolotta's direction, San Domenico restaurant in New York City received a three-star review from *The New York Times*, and *Forbes* Magazine honored the restaurant in 1990 and 1991 as the only Italian restaurant to receive four stars.

Spiaggia, Chicago's premier Italian restaurant, has been recognized with a Four Diamond Rating from the American Automobile Association (AAA) and honored with the Distinguished Restaurants of North America (DiRoNA) Award. In 1994, Bartolotta was named "Best Midwest Chef" by the James Beard Foundation.

TUSCAN MUSSEL SOUP
with White Beans

WIDE RIBBON PASTA
with Asparagus and Basil

SAUTÉED LAMB CHOPS
Glazed in Balsamic Vinegar

OVEN-FRESH RED SNAPPER
with Artichokes and Fresh Oregano

STRAWBERRIES
with Zabaione

STARBUCKS HOUSE BLEND COFFEE

appetizer / serves four

Tuscan Mussel Soup with White Beans
(*Guazzetto di Cozze e Cannellini*)

CROUTONS FOR SOUP

- 4   1-inch cubes peasant bread
- 1   clove garlic, peeled
- extra-virgin olive oil
- pinch of salt

Toast bread cubes lightly in oven until golden brown. Rub toasted croutons with garlic clove. Drizzle with olive oil and season with salt. Set aside.

MUSSEL SOUP

4	teaspoons extra-virgin olive oil
2	teaspoons butter
2	teaspoons minced garlic
2	bay leaves
48	mussels, washed
1½	cups dry white wine

pinch of crushed red pepper flakes
½ cup cannellini beans, boiled (reserve ½ cup of liquid)
4 tomatoes, blanched, seeded and diced
4 teaspoons chopped Italian parsley
salt and white pepper

In a saucepan, gently sauté minced garlic and bay leaves in oil and butter; do not brown. Add mussels, white wine and red pepper flakes. Cover, and steam open mussels. Off heat, remove mussels from pan and extract them from their shells. Set aside. Add

Wide Ribbon Pasta with Asparagus and Basil *(see page 72)*

AMERICA'S HOTTEST NEW CHEFS

the reserved cannellini bean liquid to pan. Add beans, diced tomato and chopped parsley. Add salt and white pepper to taste.

To Serve: Heat soup bowls. Place one crouton in each. Add cleaned mussels to soup, ladle over croutons and serve immediately.

entrée / serves four

Wide Ribbon Pasta with Asparagus and Basil *(Tagliatelle con Asparagi)*

PASTA

12	ounces tagliatelle pasta (ribbon pasta; recipe follows)
4	teaspoons finely chopped Italian parsley
2	teaspoons finely chopped basil
4	tablespoons extra-virgin olive oil
4	tablespoons unsalted butter
4	tablespoons grated Parmigiano-Reggiano (Parmesan) cheese
4	basil bouquets (for garnish, optional)

PASTA DOUGH

1	generous cup 'OO' Italian flour, or substitute all-purpose flour (17 ounces dry weight)
5	whole eggs, at room temperature

pinch of salt

Heap flour on a countertop and form a well in it. Crack eggs into the well and add salt. Knead for 5 minutes to form smooth dough. Allow to rest a minimum of 30 minutes. Roll very thin and cut tagliatelle ribbon noodles approximately ¼ inch wide and 12 inches long.

ASPARAGUS SAUCE

1	cup extra-virgin olive oil
4	cloves garlic, minced

Away From the Table— Ideas For Serving Coffee

Now that coffee has truly risen from the breakfast table to become a part of the tapestry of our daily lives, coffee exploration has reached an all-time high. With so many fine coffees to choose from, where to enjoy your coffee can be your next great adventure. When you entertain, make the end of the meal as eventful as its beginning. Serve coffee and dessert away from the dining table. Have you ever wished to "retire to the drawing room"? Make it simple by using a handed-down coffee service with formal, or funky, cups and saucers.

On summer evenings, enjoy dessert on the porch with iced coffee poured into milkshake glasses, topped with a dollop of whipped cream and a straw. For colder evenings, set up cushions around the fireplace and sip a Caffè Latte from thick and warm porcelain bowls. The next time you have guests over, invite them to get up from the table, and savor coffee in a different room of your house.

NICK GUNDERSON

pinch of red chili flakes
20   spears asparagus
4   whole tomatoes, peeled, seeded and diced
20   basil leaves
1   cup chicken stock

Cut asparagus thinly at a diagonal, allowing tip to remain approximately ¼ inch long. Heat olive oil in a large sauté pan at medium temperature, adding garlic and red chili flakes. Do not brown garlic. When cooked, add diced tomatoes, basil leaves, asparagus slices and chicken stock. Cook for 2 minutes at medium temperature, reducing liquid by 75 percent. Remove from heat.

To Serve: Boil tagliatelle in a large pot of salted water. Stir with a kitchen fork to prevent noodles from sticking together. When pasta is 90 percent cooked, set aside a small amount of its water, then strain pasta and add it to sauté pan containing sauce. Add parsley, basil, olive oil, butter and reserved pasta water. (Placing pasta not quite cooked in the sauce and adding a small amount of pasta water allows the pasta's natural starch to bind the sauce and the flavor of the sauce to penetrate the pasta.) Finish with freshly grated Parmigiano-Reggiano, and garnish with basil bouquets if desired.

entrée/*serves four*

Sautéed Lamb Chops Glazed in Balsamic Vinegar
(*Agnello all'Aceto Balsamico*)

POTATO-CAULIFLOWER PUREE
6   yellow potatoes
½   head cauliflower
¼   cup extra-virgin olive oil
salt and freshly ground black pepper

Boil yellow potatoes in lightly salted water. When cooked, remove from water, peel and coarsely chop. Boil cauliflower until cooked. Place both in a saucepan with olive oil and season with salt and pepper. Whip with a wooden spoon to form a chunky puree. Set aside and keep warm.

LAMB
½   cup extra-virgin olive oil
12   lamb chops, trimmed of fat (reserve scraps to make a lamb broth, if desired)
8   cloves garlic, sliced
12   sprigs rosemary (4 for garnish)
4   tablespoons unsalted butter
1   cup red wine vinegar
2   cups balsamic vinegar
½   cup tomato paste
1   cup crushed tomatoes
2   cups chicken stock or, preferably, lamb broth
salt and freshly ground black pepper

Heat at least half of the oil in a large sauté pan. Season lamb chops with salt and pepper. Sauté chops at high temperature on both sides until browned yet still very rare. Discard all cooked oil and lower temperature to medium, adding remainder of the oil,

Tuscan Mussel Soup with White Beans

sliced garlic, eight rosemary sprigs and unsalted butter. Cook until butter and garlic are both golden brown. Deglaze with red wine vinegar, balsamic vinegar, tomato paste and crushed tomatoes. Remove lamb chops when medium rare, or continue to cook to desired doneness. Set aside and keep warm.

Raise heat to high temperature and add chicken or lamb broth. Reduce sauce and add salt and pepper to taste.

To Serve: Arrange lamb chops on top of a spoonful of potato-cauliflower puree. Glaze chops with sauce and garnish each plate with a fresh rosemary sprig.

entrée / *serves four*

Oven-Fresh Red Snapper with Artichokes and Fresh Oregano
(Dentice con Carciofi all'Origano Fresco)

1	2½-pound red snapper, preferably New Zealand
1¼	cups extra-virgin olive oil
8	cloves garlic, minced
12	sprigs fresh oregano (4 for garnish)
16	small artichokes, cleaned and sliced
2	cups white wine
2	cups fish stock (made from snapper bones)
4	whole tomatoes, peeled, seeded and diced
4	teaspoons chopped Italian parsley
2	teaspoons chopped fresh oregano
4	tablespoons unsalted butter, cold

salt and black pepper

Fillet red snapper. Discard head and tail. Boil bones in water with a pinch of salt for 30 minutes to obtain a light fish broth.

Clean artichokes and slice very thin. Heat olive oil in a large sauté pan at medium temperature. Add garlic, and sauté until lightly golden but not brown. Add artichokes with eight of the whole oregano sprigs and sauté until tender. Add white wine and fish stock. Season red snapper fillets with salt and place in the pan with artichokes and broth. Oven-poach in a 375-degree oven until fish is just cooked through (approximately 5 minutes). Remove fillets and keep warm.

Remove oregano sprigs from sauce and discard. Finish sauce by reducing cooking liquid by 75 percent, adding diced tomatoes, parsley, chopped oregano and cold butter, and adjusting salt and pepper to taste.

To Serve: Place artichoke sauce at the bottom of each plate. Top with red snapper fillet, and garnish with a whole fresh oregano sprig.

dessert / *serves four*

Strawberries with Zabaione
(Fragole allo Zabaione)

STRAWBERRIES

4	cups sliced strawberries
4	teaspoons butter
4	teaspoons sugar
4	tablespoons Vin Santo, or substitute Marsala

Sauté strawberry slices in butter with sugar. Glaze with Vin Santo and place in a martini glass.

ZABAIONE

4	egg yolks
4	tablespoons Vin Santo, or substitute Marsala
4	tablespoons sugar

Place all ingredients in a double boiler over moderate heat. Whisk until frothy and shiny. Make sure heat is not so high that it scrambles the yolks.

To Serve: Pour zabaione over strawberries and serve immediately.

DECORATING

A Middle Eastern Romance

Design:
Lawrence Lake, ASID
Inter Plan Design Group
Scottsdale, Arizona

Rich tapestry, a smattering of throw pillows and simple bed linens can transform any living room into an unexpected romantic soirée. Draping material above a fireplace or over a sofa provides added texture and dimension to a room and suggests a Middle Eastern ambiance. Turn out the lights, light some candles, and lounge about your living room for an evening of decadence—here's what you'll need:

- 3 king-size white flat sheets
- A Middle Eastern-style floor rug
- Collection of large pillows
- Candles of all sizes (the more the better)
- Spray of flowers (left in plain brown wrapper)
- Material in dark or neutral colors, various sizes (optional)

Drape sofas and chairs with white sheeting. If you have a fireplace, tack a sheet up, allowing it to drape onto the mantel. Arrange folds to create additional texture. Be careful to keep material away from heat vents or the opening of the fireplace.

Additional material in dark or neutral shades provides contrast over a couch or chair. Allow cloth to drape loosely onto floor.

Pile on the pillows! Large floor pillows act as seats, and others can be scattered about the couch or on the floor.

Drape your coffee table with an area rug, runner, blanket or some interesting fabric.

Add an extensive collection of candles in varying heights along the mantel and all about the room. Brass candleholders add richness to the exotic setting.

Lay a bouquet of simple flowers on the coffee table—no need for a vase, just keep them wrapped in brown paper.

RICK TRAMONTO

Brasserie-T

Northfield, Illinois

"I wasn't interested in academics, and left two city school programs before being enrolled in a special vocational tech program. Their 'school without walls' work-study program introduced me to the basics of the culinary arts," remembers Rick Tramonto, chef and owner of Brasserie-T in Northfield, Illinois, who literally "started from scratch" in the restaurant field.

His first exposure to a strict French kitchen was at The Strathallen Hotel, in Rochester, New York, under the direction of chef and mentor Greg Broman. The Strathallen provided Tramonto with an education in the culinary arts equivalent to a master's degree. From The Strathallen Hotel, Tramonto left to work in some of New York's most popular restaurants—Tavern on The Green, The Gotham Bar & Grill, Aurora and Baton's, during which time he met his future wife, Gale Gand (a 1994 Rising Star Chef).

Tramonto and Gand teamed up and moved to The Stapleford Park Hotel in Leicestershire, England, where they received the coveted *Michelin Guide* Red "M" award for their cuisine. They were the only Americans to have won the award in seven years.

In 1993, Tramonto and Gand returned to Chicago, and, with a third partner, Henry Adaniya, opened Trio, which quickly became one of Chicago's favorite dining establishments. In 1995, Tramonto and Gand opened their new, more casual restaurant, Brasserie-T.

appetizer/*serves four*

Lobster Cocktail with Roasted Garlic Mashed Potatoes

LOBSTER

1   1½-pound lobster, live

In a pot, bring a gallon of salted water to a boil. Drop in lobster and cook 5 minutes. Place in ice water to stop cooking. When cool,

LOBSTER COCKTAIL
with Roasted Garlic Mashed Potatoes

GRILLED YELLOWFIN TUNA
with Pasta and Chinese Vegetables in Copperwell Sauce

ROASTED-HAZELNUT-AND-HERB-CRUSTED LAMB
with Five-Grain Risotto

GRILLED BEEF TENDERLOIN
with Artichoke Frittata, Curried Fried Potato Sticks and Marrow

TRIPLE CHOCOLATE ESPRESSO CANNOLI

STARBUCKS GUATEMALA COFFEE

remove shells. Cut meat into 1-inch chunks and chill.

ROASTED GARLIC MASHED POTATOES

    1½   pounds potatoes, peeled and quartered
    4   cloves garlic, roasted and peeled
    ½   cup unsalted butter
    ¼   cup heavy cream

        salt and freshly ground pepper

Bring a pot of salted water to a boil. Cook potatoes until tender. Drain. While hot, place potatoes in mixing bowl of an electric mixer with garlic, butter, cream and salt and pepper to taste. Mash with paddle attachment on low speed. If necessary, grind through food mill until smooth. Keep warm.

Triple Chocolate Espresso Cannoli *(see page 82)*

AMERICA'S HOTTEST NEW CHEFS

CILANTRO-CITRUS VINAIGRETTE

- 1 lime, juiced
- 1 lemon, juiced
- ½ orange, juiced
- 2 tablespoons extra-virgin olive oil
- 1 teaspoon chopped soft herbs (sage, parsley and basil)
- 1 teaspoon salt
- 1 teaspoon freshly ground pepper
- 1 teaspoon chopped cilantro

Whisk together all ingredients. Reserve.

GARNISH

- lobster antennas
- chives, whole
- strips of orange peel

To Serve: Toss cold lobster with cilantro-citrus vinaigrette. Place warm mashed potatoes in stemmed glasses. Top with lobster meat. Garnish each with an antenna and a chive tied with an orange-peel strip.

entrée/serves four

Grilled Yellowfin Tuna with Pasta and Chinese Vegetables in Copperwell Sauce

TUNA

- 4 6-ounce yellowfin tuna steaks
- 4 tablespoons garlic oil

Brush tuna steaks with garlic oil. Salt and pepper to taste. Grill to desired doneness.

COPPERWELL SAUCE

- ⅔ cup soy sauce
- 1 teaspoon sesame oil
- 2 tablespoons red wine vinegar
- 1 teaspoon Szechuan chili flakes
- 1¼ cups vegetable oil

Tasting Terminology

So many adjectives apply to the taste of coffee that descriptions of specific varietals and blends can begin to resemble poetry.

THE BASICS

In describing your own response to coffee-tasting experiences, it might help to bear in mind the three fundamental aspects of any coffee's taste.

Flavor—The most important tasting term describes the total impression of aroma, acidity and body. It can be used generally ("this coffee is flavorful") or with specific attributes in mind ("this coffee has a flavor reminiscent of chocolate").

Acidity—This easily misunderstood term refers to the lively, palate-cleansing property characteristic of all high-grown coffees, which is experienced primarily on the sides of the tongue. Acidity is not the same as bitterness.

Body—The tactile impression of brewed coffee in your mouth can be described as light, medium or full. Some coffees naturally have more body than others. The brewing method also affects the perception of body. Coffees made in a coffee press or an espresso machine seem fuller in body than those brewed by other methods.

TASTING TERMS

Earthy—Spicy taste "of the earth," often used to describe Indonesian coffees.

Exotic—Applied to coffees with an unusual aroma or flavor suggestive of flowers, berries or sweet spices.

Mild—Denotes coffee with harmonious flavor, such as high-grown Latin American coffees.

Tangy—Denotes a darting, pleasing brightness.

Winy—Fruit like acidity and smooth body reminiscent of fine wine.

–Exerpted from *Starbucks Passion for Coffee*

2 tablespoons brown sugar
2 tablespoons water
2 tablespoons crushed sesame seed
½ teaspoon cayenne pepper

Combine soy sauce, sesame oil, vinegar, Szechuan pepper and 1 cup of the vegetable oil in a bowl. Heat the remaining ¼ cup of oil, remove from heat, and add cayenne pepper to singe it. Add to ingredients in bowl. Heat brown sugar in water until it dissolves and caramelizes. Add to ingredients in bowl. Toast sesame seed until golden. Add to ingredients in bowl. Whisk ingredients to combine. (Recipe makes more sauce than needed for dish.)

VEGETABLES AND PASTA
½ pound linguini pasta, blanched
1 cup Chinese greens (savoy cabbage, napa cabbage, mustard greens, etc.), blanched
1 cup bok choy, blanched
1 cup snow peas, blanched
12 ears baby corn, blanched
1 cup julienned carrots, blanched
8 ounces Copperwell sauce (preceding recipe)
   salt and pepper

Reheat the linguini. Toss pasta, vegetables and sauce together, and warm over low heat. Salt and pepper to taste.

GARNISH
4 phyllo dough fans (knot phyllo dough in center, fringe ends and deep-fry)
4 tablespoons finely diced bell peppers (a tricolor mix of red, yellow and green)
4 tablespoons Szechuan oil

To Serve: Arrange one-quarter of pasta and vegetables in a decorative twist in center of each plate. Place grilled tuna off center. Garnish with fan and tricolor peppers. Drizzle with Szechuan oil.

entrée/*serves four*

Roasted-Hazelnut-and-Herb-Crusted Lamb with Five-Grain Risotto

ROASTED-HAZELNUT-AND-HERB-CRUSTED LAMB
2 tablespoons olive oil
4 lamb racks
¼ cup Dijon mustard
   hazelnut-herb coating (recipe follows)

Grilled Beef Tenderloin with Artichoke Frittata, Curried Fried Potato Sticks and Marrow

Preheat oven to 500 degrees. Heat olive oil in a sauté pan, and sear lamb on all sides. Then roast in oven for 5 minutes. Brush with mustard and pack with hazelnut-herb crumbs. Return to oven to crisp. (This makes medium-rare lamb chops.)

HERB CRUST FOR LAMB
- ⅛ bunch parsley, minced
- 2 cloves garlic, minced
- 1 tablespoon pure olive oil
- 2 cups bread crumbs
- ½ cup hazelnuts
- 2 tablespoons hazelnut oil
- salt and pepper

Heat olive oil in a small pan. Sauté garlic until tender. Put in food processor with remaining ingredients, and blend to make green crumbs.

GARLIC HERB BROTH
- 3 cloves garlic, peeled
- 3 tablespoons fresh herbs, chopped (chef uses cilantro, basil, thyme, parsley and tarragon)
- 1 quart lamb stock
- 4 tablespoons butter
- salt and pepper

Sweat garlic with 1 tablespoon of the herbs. Add lamb stock and simmer slowly. Incorporate butter, then pour through chinois. Finish by adding the remaining 2 tablespoons of herbs and salt and pepper to taste.

FIVE-GRAIN RISOTTO

For Arborio Rice:
- 1 tablespoon olive oil
- ¼ small onion, peeled and minced
- ¼ clove garlic, peeled and minced
- ½ cup Arborio rice
- 1 tablespoon white wine
- 1 cup chicken stock, boiling
- salt and pepper

For Wild Rice:
- 1 tablespoon olive oil
- ¼ small onion, peeled and minced
- ¼ clove garlic, peeled and minced
- ¼ cup wild rice
- 1 cup chicken stock, boiling
- 1 sprig thyme, finely chopped
- salt and pepper

For Barley:
- ½ cup barley
- 1 cup chicken stock

For Other Grains:
- ¼ cup red lentils, well rinsed in warm water
- 1 tablespoon flax seed

Other Ingredients:
- 1 scallion, sliced
- ½ cup sliced shiitake or cremini mushrooms
- 1 cup chicken stock, boiling
- 1 tablespoon butter
- 1 teaspoon grated Parmesan cheese
- 1 teaspoon grated Pecorino Romano cheese
- 2 tablespoons heavy cream
- 2 tablespoons chopped tomato
- 1 teaspoon chopped fresh herbs
- salt and pepper

For Arborio rice, sweat onion and garlic in olive oil in a small saucepan. Add rice and stir to coat with oil. Season with salt and pepper. Add wine and continue cooking until absorbed. Add hot stock, one ladle at a time, stirring until stock is absorbed after each addition. Set aside.

In another saucepan, heat oil and sauté garlic and onion. Add wild rice and sauté slightly. Add chicken stock, and simmer until liquid is absorbed and rice is tender. Set aside.

In another saucepan, cook barley in stock until tender.

In a round-bottomed pan, combine both cooked rices and cooked barley with lentils and flax seed. Add scallion, mushrooms and stock. Cook until tender but still *al dente*. Over medium heat, fold in butter, cheeses and cream, and salt and pepper to taste. Then fold in tomato and herbs.

To Serve: Cut crusted lamb into chops. On each plate, arrange chops on a bed of five-grain risotto. Ring with garlic herb broth.

entrée/*serves four*

Grilled Beef Tenderloin with Artichoke Frittata, Curried Fried Potato Sticks and Marrow

BEEF
- 4   6-ounce beef fillets
- 4   sprigs rosemary (for garnish)

MARINADE FOR BEEF
- ½   cup olive oil
- 1   clove garlic, chopped
- 1   sprig fresh rosemary, chopped
- 1   orange, juiced
- ⅛   teaspoon red chili flakes

Combine all ingredients. Marinate fillets in mixture for at least 2 hours or overnight.

ARTICHOKE FRITTATA
- 3   eggs
- ½   cup cream
- 1   tablespoons minced onion
- ¼   cup corn kernels
- 1   teaspoon chopped herbs (basil and parsley)
- 2   tablespoons grated Parmesan cheese
- ¼   cup chopped tomato
- ½   pound angel hair pasta, blanched
- 4   ounces baby artichokes, cleaned, quartered and blanched

salt and pepper

Whisk eggs with cream. Stir in remaining ingredients and season with salt and pepper to taste. Melt butter in a nonstick sauté pan and add frittata mixture. Cook until golden brown on one side. Flip and brown other side. Turn out onto flat surface. Cut four circles from frittata. Reserve.

CURRIED FRIED POTATO STICKS
- 2   cups canola oil
- 3   tablespoons curry powder
- 1   potato, peeled and julienned on a mandoline

Make curry oil by mixing canola oil and curry powder well and letting steep overnight.

Heat oil to 375 degrees and deep-fry potato sticks. Drain on paper towels and set aside.

RED WINE SAUCE WITH MARROW, WILD MUSHROOMS AND PROSCIUTTO
- 1   ounce bone marrow
- 1½   teaspoons olive oil
- ¼   cup *mirepoix* (carrot, onion and celery)
- 2   shallots, minced
- 1   ounce sliced white mushrooms
- ½   cup red wine
- 1½   cups veal stock
- 1   ounce julienned prosciutto
- 1   ounce wild mushrooms
- ½   teaspoon butter, plus some to finish sauce
- 1   tablespoon brandy

salt and pepper

Soak bone marrow in salted cold water for several hours or until marrow pulls away from bone easily when pushed from one side. Dice. Pass through a chinois.

In a saucepan, sweat *mirepoix*, shallots and sliced white mushrooms in olive oil. Add red wine and reduce by half. Add veal stock and again reduce by half. Add marrow and cook briefly. In another saucepan, sauté prosciutto with wild mushrooms in ½ teaspoon butter. Deglaze with brandy. Stir in reduced stock and marrow mixture. Finish sauce with butter and salt and pepper to taste.

To Serve: Grill beef tenderloin to desired doneness. Place a frittata circle on each plate. Top with a fillet. Spoon over red wine sauce. Top with curried fried potato sticks and a rosemary sprig.

dessert/serves twelve

Triple Chocolate Espresso Cannoli

Recipe by Gale Gand, pastry chef, wife and business partner of Rick Tramanto

CANNOLI TUBES

- 6 ounces dark chocolate
- 6 ounces white chocolate
- 12 pieces parchment paper, 8 by 8 inches each

Melt each type of chocolate separately over hot water, and put in squeeze bottles. Drizzle both colors of chocolate in a grid pattern onto one half of each piece of paper. Carefully roll up paper to form a tube with chocolate completely lining inside. Tape to hold position. Complete one cannoli tube at a time, keeping squeeze bottles warm. Chill to harden.

CHOCOLATE MOUSSE FILLING

- 9 ounces semisweet chocolate
- 2 tablespoons unsalted butter
- 1½ cups heavy cream
- 5 egg whites, at room temperature
- ½ cup sugar
- ¼ cup espresso, cooled

Melt chocolate and butter together. Let cool slightly. Meanwhile, whip cream and keep chilled. Warm a bowl with water and dry well. In it, whip egg whites until they become frothy. Gradually add sugar and whip until stiff and glossy. Add whites to the melted chocolate and butter by thirds, whisking well after each addition. Fold in reserved cream and cooled espresso.

Fill a pastry bag with mousse. Using a plain tip, pipe mousse into chilled cannoli tubes and freeze.

BROWN SUGAR CREAM

- 2 cups heavy cream
- 4 tablespoons brown sugar

Whip cream and sugar together into loose peaks, making sure to dissolve sugar early in the process. Divide into two equal parts.

ESPRESSO CREAM

- 1 tablespoon espresso
- half of brown sugar cream (preceding recipe)

Blend together espresso and brown sugar cream. Rewhip slightly to form loose peaks.

FRESH FRUIT SALAD

- 1 cup sugar
- 1 cup water, plus 2 tablespoons
- 1 pint raspberries
- 1½ cups sliced seasonal fruit

Make a simple syrup by boiling sugar with 1 cup of water until sugar is thoroughly dissolved. Cool. Make a raspberry puree by boiling raspberries with 2 tablespoons of water. Strain to remove pulp. Cool.

Gently combine fruit with some of the raspberry puree and some of the syrup. (More simple syrup and raspberry puree will be produced than needed for this dessert.)

To Serve: Ahead of time, cut cannoli in half and thaw slightly in refrigerator. Spoon brown sugar cream and espresso cream onto plates. Unwrap cannoli carefully and place two halves on each plate. Garnish with some fresh fruit salad.

DECORATING

A Table of Eclectic Crafts

Design:
Gail Adams, FASID
Gail Adams Interiors, Ltd.
The Mind's Eye
Arizona

A contemporary fusion of color and geometry suggests the unexpected. Shades of plum, ochre and maize mimic the stark natural beauty of a Southwestern landscape or tones of a spectacular sky at dusk. An avant-garde table complements the eccentric plating style of chef Rick Tramonto. Suggestions follow:

Oversized, hand-thrown dishes are a modern alternative to traditional china. Visit a pottery studio, home boutique or craft fair for some ideas. Large hand-painted or glazed tiles can also function as fabulous plates.

Try a runner in place of a tablecloth to highlight the beauty of a wooden or wicker tabletop. Choose a richly textured fabric and cut into two separate long strips. Hem along the edges to finish off and place one runner across the table. Overlay the second to form an "X". A single, wide runner looks splendid as well. Set dishes at each end—no placemats necessary.

Bold, contrasting colors are effective and exciting. Mix and match plates, napkins and glassware in a variety of styles to tie in with the central shades of your design.

Display round candles in terra-cotta dishes or flower pot liners. Decorate further with a collection of clay pots and small figurines set about the table.

An impressive piece of sculpture acts as a centerpiece; or substitute with a bowl of fresh vegetables such as deep-plum eggplants or green artichokes.

ALISON BARSHAK

Striped Bass
Philadelphia,
Pennsylvania

Alison Barshak, executive chef of Striped Bass in Philadelphia, is enjoying her time at the top. "You look out on a packed Saturday night and see people eating and socializing; you just stand there and say—Wow—this is unbelievable, this is what I do for a living."

Barshak has traveled the world, exploring the tastes and cultures of Europe, Mexico, South America and the United States. She spent the last 15 years gaining experience in Philadelphia kitchens, working her way up from prep cook. Barshak held positions as executive chef at the renowned Apropos and Central Bar and Grille.

To create the daily-changing, all-seafood menus at Striped Bass, Barshak expanded on her culinary expertise. "I took continuing education classes at the Culinary Institute of America, read, and went to the fish market every day," she says. *Esquire* Magazine named Striped Bass the Best New Restaurant of the Year and stated that Barshak is showing the direction for seafood cookery in the next decade.

JUMBO LUMP CRABMEAT
with Potato Pancakes, Mango and Baby Greens

TANDOORI BAKED WHOLE FISH

PARMESAN-COATED MONKFISH

THAI CURRIED SWORDFISH

CORN CRÈME BRÛLÉE
with Blueberry Polenta Cake

STARBUCKS ETHIOPIA HARRAR COFFEE

appetizer/*serves four*

Jumbo Lump Crabmeat with Potato Pancakes, Mango and Baby Greens

CRABMEAT
- 1 pound fresh jumbo lump crabmeat
- 1 mango, peeled and diced (dice 1 teaspoon finely and reserve for vinaigrette)
- 2 cups baby greens

POTATO PANCAKES
- 3 large Idaho potatoes, peeled and shredded
- 6 ounces finely diced onion
- 1 egg
- ½ teaspoon baking soda

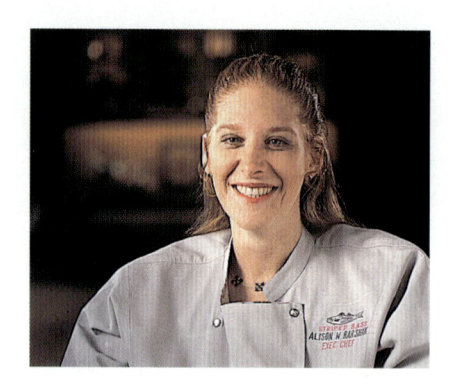

Corn Crème Brûlée with Blueberry Polenta Cake *(see page 90)*

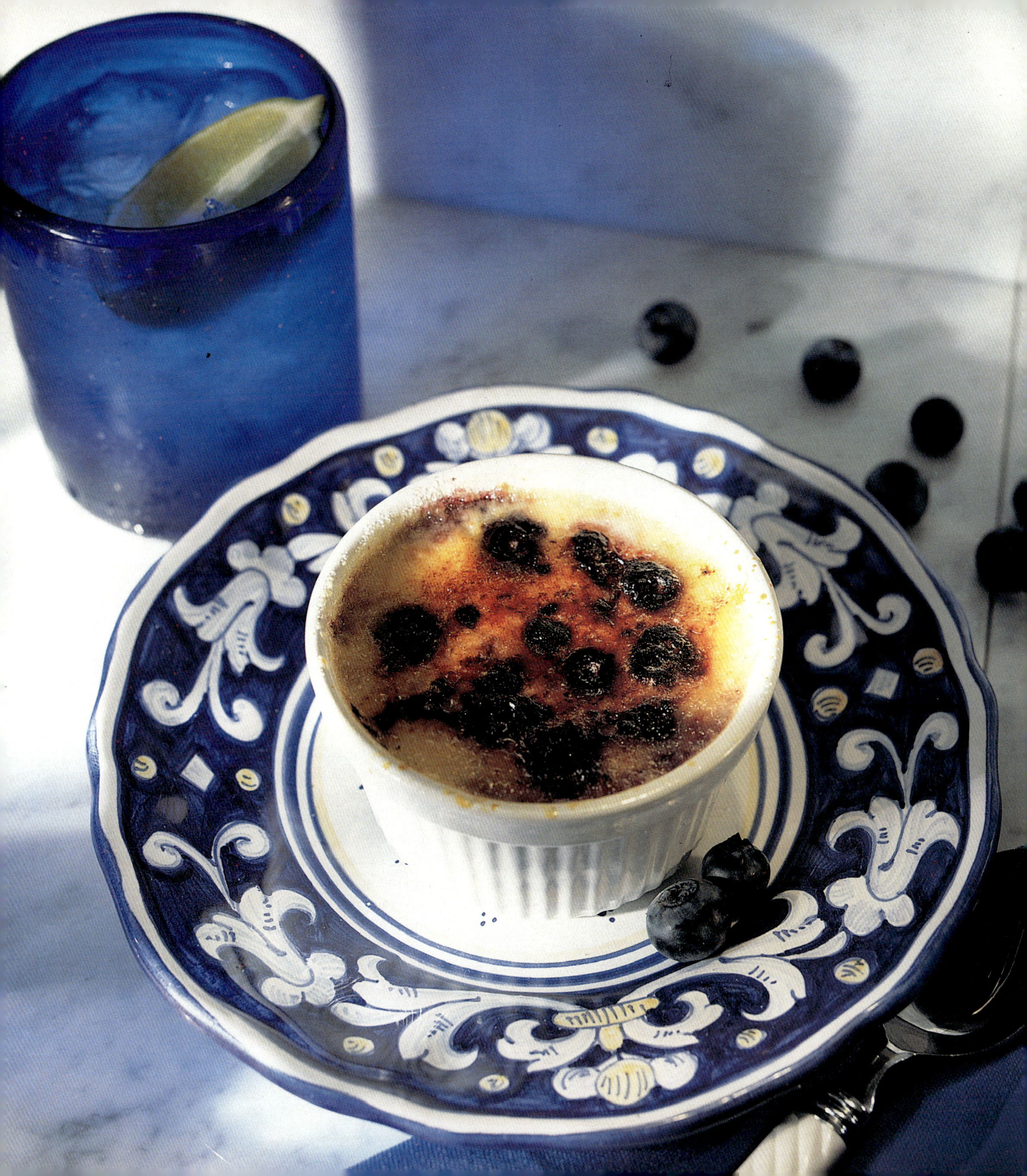

1   tablespoon flour
2   tablespoons blended oil (canola and vegetable)
     salt and pepper

Whir potato and onion in a food processor and transfer to a mixing bowl. Add eggs and baking soda. Add flour in small amounts to bind mixture. Add salt and pepper to taste.

Heat oil in a medium-size sauté pan with a screen. Place pancake mixture in pan by spoonfuls to make silver-dollar pancakes. When pancake begins to dry out at edges, turn over. Make at least 12 pancakes. This recipe will yield 20.

BRANDY CREAM

1   cup finely sliced shallots
$2/3$ cup brandy
2   cups heavy cream
     oil
     salt and pepper

Sauté shallots in oil until they begin to caramelize. Deglaze with brandy and let flame. Add cream. Reduce by half. Salt and pepper to taste.

MANGO VINAIGRETTE

2   ounces mango syrup or nectar
$1/4$ teaspoon minced jalapeño pepper
2   ounces champagne vinegar
1   teaspoon finely diced mango
4   ounces blended oil
     salt and pepper

This recipe makes more than is necessary for four servings.

Mix first five ingredients together. Do not emulsify. Salt and pepper to taste.

To Serve: Heat potato pancakes in a 350-degree oven or under a low broiler. Meanwhile, place brandy cream in a pan and add crabmeat. Taste for seasoning; add salt and pepper if necessary. Heat, and stir to coat the crab. Place diced mango on plates at ten o'clock and drizzle some vinaigrette over it. Mix a bit more of the vinaigrette with greens. Place greens on plates at two o'clock. On each plate, place a potato pancake at left below mango and scoop some of crab-cream mixture on top. Shingle another pancake next to the crab and repeat process with remaining pancakes and crab.

Exploring Espresso

The whir of the espresso machine is a welcoming sound, resulting in a brew that captures *il cuore del caffè* (the heart of the coffee). At Starbucks, a sip of this spicy, caramel-thick beverage is the concentrated result of artfully blended beans and a courageous dark roast. When brewed at home, espresso can open a world of entertaining possibilities.

Steamed milk, added to a "shot" of brewed espresso, becomes the popular *Caffè Latte*. With a topping of foamed milk, you can create the classic *Cappuccino*. Other enticing espresso variations: *Espresso Macchiato*, espresso topped with the "mark" of a spoonful of milk foam, and *Espresso con Panna*, a rich ending to a meal with its dollop of whipped cream. Add a sprinkling of spices, a splash of flavored syrup or rich chocolate to your espresso beverages, and enjoy a timeless taste of coffee.

entrée/*serves four*

Tandoori Baked Whole Fish

TANDOORI GLAZE

- 1 cup diced onion
- 1 tablespoon peeled and grated ginger
- ½ tablespoon chopped garlic
- ½ cup blended oil (canola and vegetable)
- ¼ cup dried coriander
- 1¼ tablespoons ground cumin
- 1¼ tablespoons turmeric
- 1¼ tablespoons Garam Masala (recipe follows)
- 1 teaspoon ground mace
- 1 teaspoon ground nutmeg
- 1 teaspoon ground clove
- 1 teaspoon ground black pepper
- ½ tablespoon cayenne pepper
- 1 quart plain yogurt
- ⅓ cup lemon juice

Blend onion, ginger, garlic and oil in a food processor. Add pureed mixture to spices, lemon juice and yogurt in a bowl and mix by hand. Set aside.

GARAM MASALA

- ½ cinnamon stick
- 6 or 8 black peppercorns
- 2 or 3 whole cloves
- 2 or 3 cardamom pods
- 2 or 3 coriander seeds

Combine all ingredients in a coffee mill and grind.

FISH

- 4 whole fish, approximately 1½ to 2 pounds each before cleaning (remove scales, organs and gills)
- 4 small to medium Idaho potatoes

Thai Curried Swordfish

2	large white onions
2	large red tomatoes
1	large lemon

Preheat oven to 425 degrees. Peel potatoes and cut into rounds ¼ to ½ inch thick. Peel onion and cut into ¼- to ½-inch rounds. Lightly oil bottom of a large baking dish and distribute potatoes and onions evenly. Make cross slices in flesh of fish on both sides. Place fish on top of vegetables and place 2 slices of tomato, ¼ to ½ inch thick, on top of fish. Slice lemon ¼ inch thick and place lemon slices on top of tomato slices. Cover fish and vegetables with tandoori glaze.

Place baking dish in a larger pan and pour 2 cups of water around sides of baking dish. This prevents glaze from drying out. Bake in oven for 30 to 45 minutes, or until fish is done. To test, use a knife to pull aside meat in center of fish, behind head, to see if meat is raw. Another option is to lift belly flap: if red blood is still coming from stomach cavity, cook a little longer until juices run clear.

To Serve: Remove each fish to a plate and evenly distribute onion and potato. Drizzle any sauce left in baking dish on top of fish.

entrée/*serves four*

Parmesan-Coated Monkfish

MONKFISH

4	6-ounce monkfish fillets
1	cup finely grated Parmesan cheese
1	cup finely grated bread crumbs
1	tablespoon blended oil (canola and vegetable)
	salt and pepper

Cut monkfish in half lengthwise. Place between two pieces of plastic wrap and pound out to about ¼ inch thick. Set aside. Mix bread crumbs and Parmesan cheese in a bowl. Set aside. (Cooking instructions follow other recipes.)

RISOTTO

1	cup dried porcini mushrooms
5	cups warm water
1	tablespoon blended oil (canola and vegetable)
½	cup chopped white onion
1½	cups Arborio rice
1	small bay leaf
	salt and pepper

Soak porcini mushrooms in the specified warm water for 10 minutes until soft. Remove mushrooms and chop. Save water. On medium flame, heat a 2-quart pot with oil. Add chopped onion and bay leaf. Cook until onion is translucent. Add rice and stir until grains are coated with oil. Add ½ cup of the reserved mushroom-flavored water and stir until absorbed. Keep adding liquid ½ cup at a time, allowing each addition to be absorbed, until all liquid is used. Stir after each addition of water. Cook on medium heat for about 15 minutes. Remove bay leaf. Add chopped porcinis and season with salt and pepper. Remove from heat and keep warm.

CLAM SAUCE

½	tablespoon blended oil (canola and vegetable)
1	tablespoon finely chopped garlic
½	cup white wine
1	cup chopped clams
1	cup clam broth
¼	pound butter, cut into 1-inch pieces

On medium flame, heat a small saucepan with oil. Add garlic and cook for 1 minute. Add white wine and reduce by half. Add clam broth and clams. Bring to a boil and remove from heat. Whisk in butter, a piece at a time. Set aside and keep warm.

GREMOLATA

2	tablespoons lemon zest
¼	teaspoon minced garlic

- ¼ teaspoon minced shallots
- 1½ teaspoons chopped Italian parsley
- ½ teaspoon extra-virgin olive oil

Mix all ingredients in a bowl.

To cook monkfish, remove from plastic wrap and season lightly with salt and pepper. Heat a large nonstick sauté pan with 1 tablespoon of oil on medium flame until just smoking. Coat monkfish with Parmesan bread crumbs and lay in pan. Cook until golden brown on both sides.

To Serve: Put 1 cup risotto in center of each plate. Put monkfish on top of risotto and drizzle clam sauce all over. Sprinkle with gremolata and serve.

entrée/serves four

Thai Curried Swordfish

SWORDFISH
- 4 8-ounce center-cut swordfish steaks
- 1 4-ounce can Thai red curry paste
- ½ cup blended oil (canola oil and vegetable)
- salt and pepper

In a bowl, mix Thai curry paste and oil. Salt and pepper to taste. Marinate swordfish steaks in mixture for ½ hour.

BASMATI RICE
- 1 cup Basmati rice
- 4 cups water
- salt and pepper

Boil water in a large saucepan. Add rice, and season with salt and pepper to taste. Cook rice, uncovered, until almost tender (10 to 12 minutes). Stir occasionally. Drain in a sieve and let stand until ready to use.

VEGETABLE SLAW
- 1 large red pepper, finely julienned
- ½ head savoy cabbage, shredded
- 1 large carrot, peeled and julienned
- ½ bunch scallions, thinly sliced
- 1 medium European cucumber, julienned
- ½ cup roughly chopped coriander

Mix all ingredients in a medium-sized bowl and dress with citrus vinaigrette (recipe follows).

CITRUS VINAIGRETTE
- 1 tablespoon diced shallots
- ⅓ cup freshly squeezed orange juice
- ¼ cup champagne vinegar
- ¾ cup blended oil (canola and vegetable)
- salt and pepper

Put diced shallots, orange juice and vinegar in a medium-sized bowl. Whisk in oil very slowly. Season with salt and pepper to taste.

PLANTAIN CHIPS
- 1 large green (unripe) plantain banana
- 4 cups peanut oil
- salt and pepper

Heat oil in a heavy-gauge saucepan over medium heat until oil has reached 350 degrees. Peel plantain and slice on an angle into chips ⅛ to ¼ inch thick. Drop plantain slices into oil and fry until crisp. Remove with a slotted spoon onto paper towel to drain off excess oil. Immediately sprinkle with salt and pepper to taste. Let sit to cool.

COCONUT-LEMONGRASS SAUCE
- 1 teaspoon blended oil (canola and vegetable)
- ½ tablespoon minced garlic
- ½ tablespoon grated ginger
- 3 stalks lemongrass, smashed and cut into ¼-inch pieces
- ½ cup white wine
- 1 cup coconut milk

1	cup Coco Lopez cocktail mixer		6	egg yolks
2	teaspoons Thai red curry paste			vanilla extract
⅓	teaspoon Chinese five-spice powder		1	cup blueberries
1	tablespoon lime juice			
	salt and pepper			

Preheat oven to 350 degrees. Line bottom of a 9-inch square cake pan and spray with cooking spray. Combine flour, cornmeal and baking powder and set aside. Cream butter and sugar until light and fluffy. Add eggs, egg yolks and vanilla to taste to the butter and sugar mixture in three stages, scraping bowl after each addition. Add dry ingredients until well incorporated. Fold in blueberries. Pour batter into prepared pan. Bake for about 20 minutes, or until cake springs to the touch or a knife inserted comes out clean.

In a 1-quart saucepan, heat oil on medium temperature. Add garlic, lemongrass and ginger. Cook for 1 to 2 minutes. Deglaze with wine and reduce by half. Add coconut milk, cocktail mixer, Thai curry paste and Chinese spice. Whisk together and bring to a boil, then turn down to a simmer. Cook down until sauce is thick (about 5 to 10 minutes). Add lime juice and season with salt and pepper.

To Serve: Make a shallow mound of vegetable slaw dressed with citrus vinaigrette on center of each plate (about 1½ cups per serving). Push out to sides to form a center well for Basmati rice. Grill swordfish to desired doneness. Heat rice in a sauté pan with a little water to steam. Place about 1 cup of rice per plate in center of slaw. Place grilled swordfish on top of rice. Ladle coconut-lemongrass sauce over fish and around outside of slaw. Garnish with plantain chips.

dessert/*serves four*

Corn Crème Brûlée with Blueberry Polenta Cake

POLENTA CAKE

¾	cup all-purpose flour, plus 1 tablespoon
½	cup yellow cornmeal, plus 1 tablespoon
2½	teaspoons baking powder
1⅔	cups unsalted butter
1	cup granulated sugar
3	whole eggs

CORN CRÈME BRÛLÉE BASE

1	quart heavy cream
1	ear fresh sweet corn
10	egg yolks
¾	cup granulated sugar
2	cups fresh blueberries

Remove corn kernels from cob and reserve. Place cream and corn cob in a heavy-bottomed saucepan and place over medium heat. Scald cream; do not boil. In a stainless-steel bowl, combine egg yolks and sugar. Blend yolk/sugar mixture into cream. Strain mixture and cob. Place bowl in an ice bath to cool. Fold in blueberries. (This recipe makes extra crème brûlée base.)

Preheat oven to 300 degrees. Cut four circles of polenta cake to fit into 2-inch-wide ramekins. Place cake in bottom of each ramekin. Sprinkle reserved corn kernels onto cake. Fill remainder of ramekin with crème brûlée base. Bake in a water bath for 20 to 30 minutes, until a knife inserted comes out clean. Cool, but serve at room temperature.

To Serve: Sprinkle tops with sugar and place under broiler until caramelized. (This will not take long, so watch carefully.)

A Tropical Rendezvous

You can almost hear the sultry rhythm of steel drums and the whisper of a tropical breeze at this exotic Caribbean gala. A bold copper cloth radiates with warmth and sets the stage for the lush palm tree centerpiece cascading with colorful island fruits. Following are the materials and instructions to recreate this whimsical setting:

- 25 palm fronds
- Approximately 1 yard of "Commodore" burlap
- 28" to 30" PVC pipe or Plexiglas pipe
- Oasis (floral foam) bouquet holder (used to create bridal bouquets)
- 1 block floral foam, pre-soaked in water
- A 12" to 14" round plastic tray
- Floral tape
- Ti leaves or any tropical-looking leaves
- Spanish moss
- Various tropical fruit, such as pineapple, oranges, limes, mangos
- Long toothpicks
- Iridescent angel dust or glitter (optional)

CREATING THE BASE

Begin by cutting a block of Oasis foam to fit the 12" or 14" tray. Place foam in tray and secure by wrapping with floral tape in a criss-cross pattern over the top and affixing to bottom of tray. Add water.

Bend ti leaves to form a loop and anchor both ends into floral foam. Continue adding looped leaves evenly until most of base is covered. Allow room for fruit to be added later.

CREATING THE PALM TREE

Cut PVC pipe to desired height (28" to 30"). Cut burlap into several long, thin strips. Tape end of strip to bottom of pipe and wrap diagonally along and secure at top. Continue wrapping pipe with two or three strips until entire surface is covered. This should simulate a palm tree trunk.

Pre-soak floral foam and place handle into top of pipe or "trunk." Wrap with tape to fasten. Stick palm fronds into floral foam and arrange to imitate palm leaves. Fill in gaps between greens with Spanish moss. Mist leaves with water. For a shimmery effect, lightly sprinkle iridescent glitter onto palm leaves.

Next, secure "tree" by pushing trunk or pipe into floral foam in base tray. To finish, gather variety of colorful fruits and arrange in among looped ti leaves at base of trunk. Secure fruits in place by skewering with long toothpicks and positioning in floral foam. Smaller fruits such as strawberries and lemons can be used whole. Larger fruits such as oranges and pineapples may be cut in half and secured so that the uncut half faces outward.

Remaining palm fronds and fruit may be arranged loosely around the bottom of the arrangement to complete the tropical theme.

LEMON LEAF VOTIVES

- Small glass votive holders with candles
- Several branches of lemon leaf or any sturdy attractive leaf
- Double-sided tape
- Raffia or straw

Wrap a strip of double-sided tape around top and bottom of votive holder.

Pull individual leaves off branches and stick back of leaf vertically or at a slight angle onto holder (pointed end up). Continue applying leaves around votive until covered.

Trim excess leaves so they are flush with the bottom of the holder. To finish, wrap a strand of raffia over leaves at center and tie off in a knot. Silk leaves can be substituted for fresh.

Design: Larry Gaines and Don Patt, Potts by Patt of San Diego

PAUL O'CONNELL

Providence
Brookline, Massachusetts

"I was looking at a travel magazine one day and saw a picture of an old Labrador retriever sitting outside a quaint country restaurant in France called La Providence. It evoked something wonderful inside me, and I thought the name 'Providence' (meaning "guided by the divine hand of nature") was a perfect name for a restaurant where I could draw on the natural foods of my region," recalls Paul O'Connell, executive chef and owner of—you guessed it—Providence, in Brookline, Massachusetts. His dream was to open a casual restaurant that brings back some of the small comforts that have been lost in our daily lives.

O'Connell studied at Johnson and Wales Culinary University, and under such noted chefs as Lydia Shire of The Parker House in Boston, Jasper White of Jasper's, Chris Schlesinger of the East Coast Grill in Cambridge (where O'Connell first became a sous chef), and most recently, under Todd English of Olives (a 1994 America's Rising Star Chef). From it all, O'Connell has created a style that is uniquely his.

O'Connell uses his cooking skills to raise money for numerous charitable events across the country, and he contributes to programs such as Meals on Wheels and Aid & Comfort. He has also served as a board member of the American Institute of Wine and Food.

BIBB AND WATERCRESS SALAD
with Hot Mustard, Toasted Walnut Bread and Blue Goat Cheese

WOOD-GRILLED DOUBLE-CUT PORK CHOPS
with Colcannon-Style Mashed Potatoes

WOOD-GRILLED QUAIL
with Spiced Cranberry and Persimmon Glaze and a Pilaf of Quinoa and Red Lentils

VEAL PASTRAMI

NEW ENGLAND BLUEBERRY CAKE AND STONE-GROUND WHITE CORNMEAL COOKIES
with Summer Berries and Farm Cream

STARBUCKS KENYA COFFEE

appetizer / serves four to six

Bibb and Watercress Salad with Hot Mustard, Toasted Walnut Bread and Blue Goat Cheese

SALAD

- 2 heads Bibb lettuce
- 1 bunch watercress
- 1 head endive
- 6 ounces domestic blue goat cheese

walnut bread, cut into 12 large dice and toasted lightly

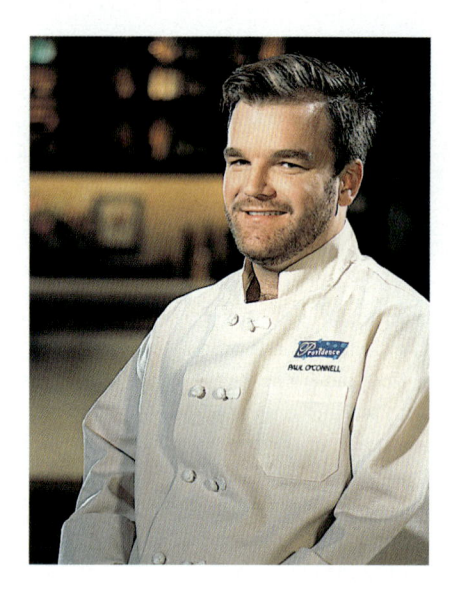

Wood-Grilled
Double-Cut
Pork Chops with
Colcannon-Style
Mashed Potatoes
(see page 94)

Coffee, Wine and Foods

Experimenting with combinations of foods and coffees is a great deal like pairing foods and wines. The following guidelines can help in building a menu of coffee, wine and foods that complement each other.

Fruit and Spice
Contrast the fruitiness of a red Rhone with the spice of Arabian Mocha Java or Gold Coast Blend.® Enhances the flavors of red meats, chicken, and exotic ethnic dishes.

Fruit and Bouquet
Balance the cherry-like, earthy Sangiovese with aromatic Arabian Mocha Sanani. Serve with heartier fishes, chicken, shellfish and pork.

Heavyweights
Parallel the currant-like flavors of a Cabernet or Merlot with the floral taste of Kenya or the heavy body of Sumatra. Perfect with red meats, pork and pasta.

Fruit and Flowers
Desserts accompanied by fruity late-harvest wines are complemented by our African coffees. Try a floral Ethiopia Sidamo or a rich, bright Kenya.

Acidity and Balance
Match a fine, crisp Chardonnay with our mellow Colombia Nariño Supremo. A great accompaniment to chicken and grilled vegetable dishes.

¼ cup sliced red onion

Wash and spin dry the Bibb and watercress. Set aside in a cool place. To make croutons, arrange walnut bread slices on a cookie sheet. Cut endive in half lengthwise, then into thin strips. Arrange endive on walnut bread. Crumble blue cheese over endive. Set aside.

DRESSING

½ cup sour cream
2 teaspoons Dijon mustard
2 teaspoons dry mustard
1 teaspoon Worcestershire sauce
½ teaspoon cayenne pepper
¼ cup lemon juice
½ cup olive oil
salt and pepper

In a large mixing bowl, whisk together sour cream, mustards, Worcestershire sauce and cayenne pepper. Add lemon juice and olive oil while steadily whisking. Thin with a little water if desired. Season with salt and pepper.

To Serve: To assemble salad, place desired amount of dressing in a large bowl. Add Bibb lettuce, watercress and red onion, and toss until lightly coated. Heat walnut bread croutons in a 350-degree oven until cheese begins to melt. Remove from oven. Arrange two or three croutons on each plate. Place salad carefully in the center.

entrée/*serves six*

Wood-Grilled Double-Cut Pork Chops with Colcannon-Style Mashed Potatoes

PORK CHOPS

6 10-ounce pork rib chops
1 gallon water

Bibb and Watercress Salad with Hot Mustard, Toasted Walnut Bread and Blue Goat Cheese

1	onion, sliced
4	cloves garlic, crushed
3	bay leaves
¼	cup molasses
1	tablespoon sea or kosher salt
1	tablespoon cumin
1	tablespoon coriander
1	tablespoon red pepper flakes
1	tablespoon fennel seed

Mix water, onion, garlic, molasses and seasonings together in a 3-gallon plastic container. Submerge pork chops in this brine and refrigerate for 24 hours.

ONION SAUCE

2	tablespoons olive oil
½	cup diced leeks
½	cup chipolene onions, peeled
½	cup baby red onions, peeled
2	cups Sauternes or sweet wine
1	bay leaf
2	cups veal stock
2	tablespoons chopped thyme
	salt and pepper

Heat a heavy-bottomed 3-quart saucepan. Add oil, leeks, and chipolene and red onions. Cook over

95

medium heat, stirring frequently, until onions begin to brown. Add sweet wine and bay leaf, and reduce by two-thirds. Add veal stock and thyme, and simmer over low heat for 20 minutes. Remove from heat. Adjust seasoning and set aside.

COLCANNON-STYLE MASHED POTATOES

4	russet potatoes, peeled
1	cup cubed rutabaga turnip
4	tablespoons butter
½	cup heavy cream
1	cup sliced savoy cabbage
½	cup sour cream
	salt and pepper

Place potatoes and diced rutabaga in a large pot, and cover with cold water. Bring to a boil. Cook until potatoes are done. Drain. In a heavy-bottomed pot, heat butter and heavy cream to a boil. Add savoy cabbage and sour cream. Toss until cabbage is wilted. Remove from heat. Place all ingredients in a stainless-steel bowl, and mash together. Season to taste with salt and pepper.

To Serve: Prepare a charcoal or gas grill for medium heat. Remove pork chops from brine. Grill chops on one side until marked. Turn over. When second sides are marked, move to low heat. Grill until meat is cooked through. On each plate, spoon colcannon-style potatoes next to pork chop and ladle onion sauce over meat.

entrée/*serves six*

Wood-Grilled Quail with Spiced Cranberry and Persimmon Glaze and a Pilaf of Quinoa and Red Lentils

QUAIL

6	quail, semiboneless
	olive oil
	salt and pepper
	watercress (for garnish)

Season quail with salt and pepper. Set aside.

PERSIMMON-CRANBERRY GLAZE

2	tablespoons canola oil
2	tablespoons diced shallots
3	tablespoons minced ginger
2	teaspoons cardamom
2	tablespoons persimmon pulp
½	cup cranberries
½	cup balsamic vinegar
¼	cup honey
½	cup chicken stock
	salt and pepper

Heat a sauté pan over high heat. Add canola oil, shallots and ginger. Then add cardamom and toss. When shallots are transparent, add persimmon pulp and cranberries. Then add vinegar, honey and chicken stock. Simmer for 5 minutes. Adjust seasoning and remove from heat.

QUINOA AND RED LENTIL PILAF

2	lemons, halved
2	bay leaves
2	teaspoons salt
¾	cup quinoa
1	cup red lentils
½	cup olive oil
¼	cup minced scallion
¼	cup minced red pepper
2	tablespoons chopped thyme
2	tablespoons chopped parsley
	salt and pepper

Fill two 2-quart saucepans with water and heat to a boil. To each pan add half of one lemon, one bay leaf and 1 teaspoon of salt. Add quinoa to one pan and red lentils to the other. Cook red lentils until al dente (about 10 minutes). Strain, and rinse to cool. The quinoa will take about 15 minutes to cook. It is done when grain splits. Rinse under cold water in a fine strainer.

Heat olive oil in a large sauté pan. Add scallion and red pepper. Toss. Add cooked lentils and quinoa, and toss frequently. Add thyme and parsley. Season to taste with salt, pepper and a squeeze of juice from the remaining lemon.

To Serve: Prepare a gas or charcoal grill for high heat. Brush seasoned quail lightly with olive oil and place breast side down on the hottest part of the grill. Grill until golden brown, moving birds two or three times. Flip quail over and grill for 2 to 3 minutes. Brush some of the persimmon-cranberry glaze on breast side while cooking.

Put warm pilaf in the center of each plate. Place quail on pilaf, and dollop persimmon-cranberry glaze on quail. Garnish with watercress.

entrée/*serves twenty to twenty-four*
Veal Pastrami

CURING BRINE

4	tablespoons sea or kosher salt
½	cup sweet paprika
½	cup cracked coriander seed
¼	cup mace
1	cup granulated sugar
2	cups pureed onions
¼	cup pureed fresh garlic
2	gallons water

Place all ingredients in a non-reactive (glass or plastic) 5-gallon container. Mix well.

VEAL

1	12-pound veal breast, boned (trimmed weight is about 6 pounds; reserve bones)
1	cup kosher salt
1	cup freshly cracked black pepper
1	cup cracked coriander seed
¼	cup sweet paprika
2	tablespoons ground mace
1	pint whole-grain mustard
	fried julienned potatoes (for garnish)

Place trimmed veal breast in brine, making sure it is completely submerged. Cover container. Place in refrigerator 36 hours to cure.

To cook, prepare a smoker with applewood chips and heat to about 250 degrees. Remove veal from brine, and drain on rack placed over sheet pan. Combine salt, pepper, paprika and mace in a nonreactive bowl. Mix well. Sprinkle, rub and press this mixture onto all sides of veal breast. Place rack with breast in smoker, and smoke for 3 hours. Transfer to refrigerator and let cool for 6 hours.

Heat oven to 350 degrees. Place veal and rack in roasting pan filled with water to a depth of 1 inch. Cover with foil. Braise 1 hour, or until done. Remove from pan and let cool.

VEAL JUS

6	pounds (approximately) veal breast bones, brushed with vegetable oil
3	cups *mirepoix* (1 part celery, 2 parts onion, 2 parts carrot)
4	cups dry white wine
4	cups sweet vermouth
3	bay leaves
4	sprigs fresh thyme
4	sprigs parsley
¼	cup black peppercorns
2	gallons cold water

Heat oven to 450 degrees. Put veal bones in roasting pan, and place in oven. Roast until bones are golden brown. Transfer bones to large stockpot over medium heat. Add *mirepoix*, wine, vermouth, bay leaves, thyme, parsley and peppercorns. Bring to a boil and reduce by half. Adjust heat to medium. Add water and bring to a boil. Simmer 4 hours, skimming as needed. Strain into clean saucepan through fine chinois. Return to stove in new pan. Reduce to 1 quart. Reserve and keep warm.

To Serve: Slice cold pastrami into ¼-inch slices. Warm in veal *jus*. Transfer to warm plates. Garnish with potatoes and additional warm veal *jus* thickened with a little of the whole-grain mustard. Pass more mustard on the side.

dessert/*serves twelve*

New England Blueberry Cake and Stone-Ground White Cornmeal Cookies with Summer Berries and Farm Cream

(This recipe was developed by Janet Martinez.)

BLUEBERRY CAKES

1¼	cups cake flour
¼	teaspoon baking soda
¼	teaspoon cream of tartar
¼	teaspoon salt
2	eggs
¾	cup sugar, plus some for pan
¾	cup heavy cream
1	pint New England blueberries (reserve ¼ pint for garnish)

lemon syrup (recipe follows)
parchment paper

Preheat oven to 325 degrees. Sift together flour, baking soda, cream of tartar and salt three times. Measure out ¼ cup and reserve. In another bowl, mix together eggs and sugar very well. In another bowl, whip heavy cream to soft peaks. Fold cream into egg mixture by stages, alternating with dry ingredients. Add the reserved ¼ cup of dry mix to blueberries and gently fold in; do not overmix. Prepare a tin with twelve 2-inch muffin cups by lining with buttered parchment paper disks and sugar. Spoon batter into cups and bake for 12 to 15 minutes. When cool, brush cakes with lemon syrup.

LEMON SYRUP

1	cup sugar
1	cup water
1	tablespoon lemon zest

Combine sugar and water in a 2-quart saucepan and bring to a boil. Add lemon zest. Simmer for 10 to 15 minutes. Remove from heat and let cool.

WHITE CORN COOKIES

⅔	cup all-purpose flour
¾	cup 10X (superfine) sugar
¾	cup white corn meal
8	tablespoons butter
¾	cup honey
2	egg whites

Preheat oven to 350 degrees. Mix together flour, sugar and cornmeal. In another bowl, beat butter to soft peaks. Add honey to butter and continue to beat. Add egg whites and continue to beat until small lumps form. Add dry ingredients and beat until mixture is smooth. Drop by tablespoons onto a cookie sheet coated with a nonstick spray. Bake until golden. Yield is about a dozen cookies.

WHIPPED FARM CREAM

3	ounces white chocolate, chopped
2	cups heavy cream
½	teaspoon vanilla

In a saucepan, scald heavy cream and vanilla. Pour over white chocolate. Strain and cool. Using a hand whisk, whip heavy cream mixture over ice until stiff.

To Serve: Place a cake on each plate. Spoon farm cream beside cake. Stick a cookie in the cream at an angle. Garnish with reserved blueberries.

DECORATING

A Bountiful Harvest

Design:
Diane B. Worth, ASID
The Carlton Connection
Joan Baron, tile artist
Scottsdale, Arizona

A traditional New England-style banquet set with antique silver and china handed lovingly down through the generations is the inspiration for this charming affair. Family heirlooms set over an old-fashioned lace cloth suggest the innocence of an earlier time. Capture the romance of the past with the following suggestions:

Choose a china pattern to set the mood, and carry out its pattern by selecting colors and flowers to match. A grapevine pattern is complemented by adding fresh grapevines to the table. Elegant silver goblets hold grapes for each place setting.

Pick flowers from your garden and highlight them in an antique water pitcher or china bowl. A pewter platter serves as an underlay for the centerpiece and reflects candlelight.

Set out a variety of pewter or silver candlesticks and select a soft shade of candles to match your bouquet.

Lay out a variety of delicate teacups and cut crystal to hold cinnamon sticks and chocolate swirls.

Personalize your table by marking each place setting with a wooden Scrabble rack with tiles spelling out the guest's name.

Simmer some potpourri on the stove before guests arrive to enhance the homey atmosphere.

MATTHEW KENNEY

Matthew's
New York, New York

"The greatest joy is seeing the end result—and knowing that you made it," says Matthew Kenney, executive chef and partner of Matthew's in New York City. The Connecticut-born Kenney grew up in Maine and developed a love for nature and a respect for all things natural and healthful.

Kenney planned on becoming a lawyer, but after graduating from the University of Maine he became enamored with the energy surrounding New York restaurants. After he graduated from the French Culinary Institute in 1990, Kenney's appetite for knowledge and experience brought him to the kitchens of Malvasia, La Caravelle and Alo Alo restaurants, and then Banana Café, where he was executive chef.

In the fall of 1993, Kenney opened Matthew's, where he is both executive chef and owner, and where his love of fresh herbs and spices is reflected in his New Mediterranean cuisine.

In addition to earning him the 1994 and 1995 nomination for Rising Star Chef by the James Beard Foundation, Kenney's gentle approach and keen attention to detail have also been recognized by *Food & Wine* Magazine, which named him one of 1994's "Ten Best New Chefs in America."

Due to have opened in August, 1995 is Kenney's Bar Anise, a casual Mediterranean café in New York focusing on the foods inspired from Mexico, Egypt, Greece, Spain and Italy. Also in the works is Kenney's first cookbook.

AHI TUNA TARTARE
with Fennel, Caraway Toast and Green Olive Tapénade

CRISPY RED SNAPPER
with Eggplant Agrodolce

LEMON CHICKEN
with Moroccan Olives, Pine Nuts, Toasted Garlic and Couscous

CORIANDER-CRUSTED VENISON
with Spice-Glazed Sweet Potato

CHERRY SOUP
with Fromage Blanc

STARBUCKS KENYA COFFEE

appetizer/*serves four*
Ahi Tuna Tartare with Fennel, Caraway Toast and Green Olive Tapénade

TUNA

8	ounces sushi-grade tuna, very fresh
1	tablespoon grated lemon peel

Ahi Tuna Tartare with Fennel, Caraway Toast and Green Olive Tapénade

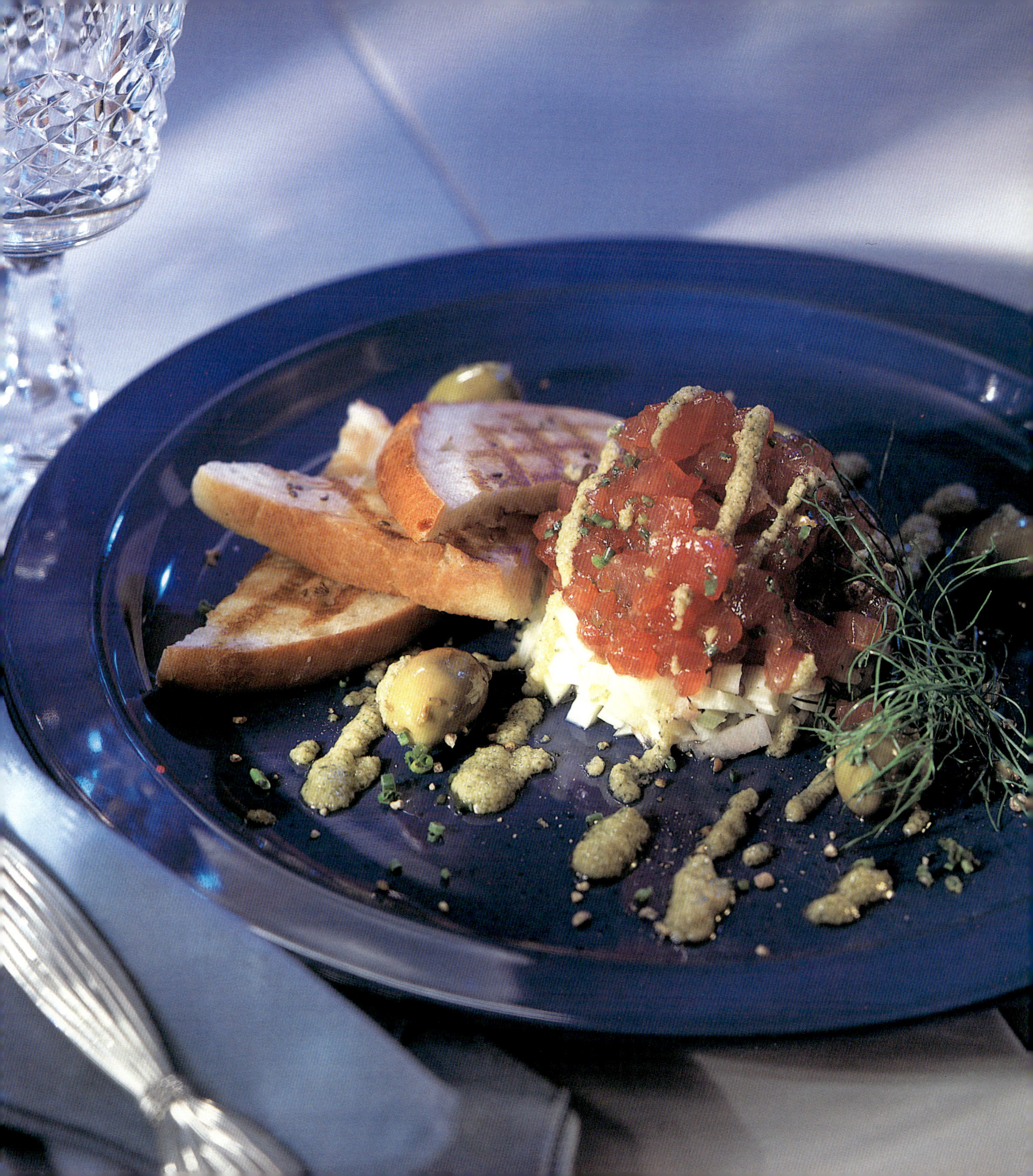

AMERICA'S HOTTEST NEW CHEFS

Coffee and Tea

Tea flavor characteristics, like those of coffee, vary widely according to growing region, altitude, climate and processing technique. A bit of exploration into the realm of tea uncovers insights that parallel those of the coffee world.

Like our coffees, our Infusia™ teas offer many different tastes, ranging from bright to floral to exotically spicy. For delicately flavored or lighter dishes, a scented or green tea like Jasmine or Earl Grey is a delightful companion. A heavier dish can be balanced with the crisp, tannic quality of a hearty black tea blend, such as English Breakfast or the piquant Chai Spice.

Coffee or tea—the eternal after-dinner question. With coffee, your experience is rich and full, with deep flavors that linger far beyond dessert. Choose tea, and end your meal with an aromatic and exotic taste that gently guides you into the evening.

1 tablespoon olive oil
1 teaspoon light soy sauce
3 tablespoons minced chives
Tabasco hot pepper sauce
salt and pepper

Dice tuna into $1/8$-inch cubes with a very sharp knife (to keep knife clean, rub frequently on a lightly oiled towel). With a spoon, mix diced tuna with lemon peel, oil, soy sauce and chives in a small bowl. Add a dash of Tabasco and season with salt and pepper. This can be prepared up to one hour in advance.

FENNEL

1 bulb fennel, with sprigs, washed
2 tablespoons lemon juice
1 tablespoon sherry vinegar
½ teaspoon freshly ground coriander seeds
1 tablespoon minced shallots
½ cup walnut oil
salt and pepper

Pull apart fennel bulb and dice the pieces. Combine lemon juice, sherry vinegar, ground coriander seeds, shallots and walnut oil. Season to taste with salt and pepper. Dress fennel with this mixture.

CARAWAY TOAST

4 slices brioche
1 teaspoon butter
1 teaspoon ground caraway seeds, toasted
pinch of salt

Mix butter with caraway seeds and salt. Spread on brioche, grill, and cut slices into quarters.

TAPÉNADE

2 ounces green picholine olives, pitted
1 anchovy fillet
1 teaspoon small capers
1 teaspoon lemon juice

¼ teaspoon anise seed, toasted
4 tablespoons olive oil
water to thin, as needed
coarse salt and freshly ground pepper

Puree olives, anchovy and capers in a blender or food processor. Add lemon juice. While machine is running, add oil and water and puree until smooth. Season with salt and pepper to taste. Force through a strainer and set aside.

GARNISH

sliced green picholine olives
cracked pepper
minced chives and fennel sprigs

To Serve: On four individual plates, place a serving of fennel in the middle and top with seasoned tuna. Spoon a little tapénade on each plate and on tuna. Garnish with olives, cracked pepper, chives and fennel sprigs.

Crispy Red Snapper with Eggplant Agrodolce

entrée/*serves four*
Crispy Red Snapper with Eggplant Agrodolce

RED PEPPER JUICE
- 4 red bell peppers
- 1 teaspoon paprika
- 2 tablespoons butter
- salt and cayenne pepper

Remove seeds from bell peppers. Cut peppers into 1-inch pieces. Puree in a food processor, then strain through a cheesecloth. Measure out 1 cup of resulting juice. Add paprika. Reduce by two-thirds and finish with butter, salt and cayenne to taste. Set aside.

EGGPLANT
- 1 sweet onion, chopped
- 1 large eggplant, diced, salted and drained
- 2 tablespoons balsamic vinegar
- 4 tablespoons blanched orange zest
- 4 tablespoons orange juice
- 4 tablespoons pine nuts
- 1 tablespoon sugar
- pinch of crushed red pepper flakes
- 2 tablespoons chopped chives
- salt and pepper
- olive oil

Heat a heavy skillet and sweat onions in olive oil until translucent. Add eggplant and sauté until soft and golden. Deglaze with orange juice and vinegar, and cook away liquid. Add orange zest, pine nuts, pepper flakes and sugar. Salt and pepper to taste. Add chives.

POTATOES
- 8 fingerling potatoes, boiled
- 2 teaspoons chopped parsley
- 1 tablespoon butter
- 1 tablespoon chicken stock
- salt and pepper

Warm potatoes with butter, stock, parsley and salt and pepper to taste.

RICE FLOUR BATTER FOR SNAPPER
- ½ cup rice flour
- ½ cup water
- 2 tablespoons baking powder
- salt and cayenne pepper

Mix ingredients, adding salt and cayenne to taste.

RED SNAPPER
- 2 tablespoons canola oil
- 4 5- to 6-ounce red snapper fillets, skins on
- 1 cup rice flour batter (preceding recipe)

Preheat oven to 400 degrees. Heat oil in a heavy nonstick skillet. Dip fish fillets in rice flour batter and cook on stove, skin side first, until golden brown. Finish for 3 minutes in oven.

To Serve: Place potatoes on a plate. Top with fish. Add eggplant mixture and drizzle with red pepper reduction.

entrée/*serves four*
Lemon Chicken with Moroccan Olives, Pine Nuts, Toasted Garlic and Couscous

CHICKEN
- 2 3-pound chickens
- 2 tablespoons olive oil
- salt and pepper
- chopped chives, scallions or cilantro leaves (for garnish)

MARINADE FOR CHICKEN
- ½ cup olive oil
- 2 lemons, juiced (use Moroccan preserved lemons, chopped, if available)
- ½ tablespoon roughly chopped cilantro leaves
- 2 teaspoons freshly chopped ginger
- pinch of crushed red pepper flakes
- 1 teaspoon freshly ground white pepper

Mix ingredients and coat chickens. Cover and marinate in refrigerator for 6 to 24 hours.

Preheat oven to 375 degrees. Season chickens with salt and pepper inside and out and truss. Heat ovenproof roasting pan over high heat on stove. Add olive oil. Brown chickens in pan until golden on all sides. Place in oven and roast for 50 minutes or until juices are pale yellow. Remove chickens from roasting pan and set aside. Pour fat out of pan, reserving about 3 tablespoons for sauce (recipe follows).

MOROCCAN OLIVE AND PINE NUT SAUCE
- 3 tablespoons melted chicken fat (from roasted chicken)
- 5 tablespoons grated white onion
- 1 tablespoon minced ginger
- 1 teaspoon minced garlic
- pinch of crushed red pepper flakes
- pinch of saffron
- ⅓ cup sliced Moroccan green olives
- ⅓ cup pine nuts, toasted
- 3 tablespoons lemon juice
- 3 tablespoons honey
- 1 quart chicken stock, reduced to 2 cups
- 2 tablespoons butter
- 1 teaspoon chopped fresh parsley
- 1 tablespoon chopped cilantro leaves
- salt and pepper

To the 3 tablespoons of fat left in pan after chicken is roasted, add grated onion, garlic and ginger and cook until onion just begins to brown. Add crushed red pepper, saffron, olives and pine nuts, and deglaze with lemon juice. Add honey and reduced chicken stock, and reduce by half. Finish sauce with butter, parsley, cilantro and salt and pepper to taste. Reserve, keeping warm.

COUSCOUS
- 2 cups chicken stock
- 2 cups medium-grain couscous
- 1 medium carrot, cut into ¼-inch cubes
- ½ red bell pepper, seeded and diced
- ½ onion, diced
- ½ zucchini, cut to ¼-inch dice
- 1 tablespoon turmeric
- 4 tablespoons fresh chopped parsley
- pinch of saffron

Bring chicken stock to a simmer. In a large sauté pan, sweat carrot, red pepper, onion and zucchini until tender. Add saffron, turmeric and stock. Place dry couscous in a large bowl and pour vegetable stock mixture over it. Stir to combine. Cover with plastic wrap and let stand approximately 15 minutes.

To Serve: Brown chickens further under broiler if necessary. Remove trussing and carve. (Chickens can be served whole.) Serve with couscous. Drizzle sauce over chicken, and garnish with chopped chives, scallions or cilantro leaves.

entrée/*serves four*

Coriander-Crusted Venison with Spice-Glazed Sweet Potato

VENISON
- 4 6-ounce boneless venison loin steaks
- 2 teaspoons cracked white peppercorns
- 4½ teaspoons cracked coriander seeds
- 5 allspice berries, crushed
- 1 cinnamon stick

2 cups Pinot Noir wine
1 cup squab, venison or beef glacé (stock reduction)
butter
kosher salt
fresh cilantro (for garnish)

Roll venison in pepper and 4 teaspoons of the cracked coriander seeds. For sauce, add allspice, cinnamon and the remaining ½ teaspoon of coriander seeds to wine and reduce by 90 percent. Add glacé and reduce by half. Finish with butter and salt.

SPICE-GLAZED SWEET POTATO

4 tablespoons butter
½ teaspoon ground ginger
½ teaspoon nutmeg
½ teaspoon cinnamon
½ teaspoon cumin
2 sweet potatoes
salt and cayenne pepper

Preheat oven to 400 degrees. Melt butter and mix in spices (salt and pepper to taste). Set aside. Clean skin of sweet potatoes. Cut potatoes in half lengthwise and bake for 15 minutes. Brush with butter-spice mixture and continue baking until cooked through, brushing with additional butter if desired.

VEGETABLES

2 cups fava beans
20 to 30 asparagus spears

Blanch separately in boiling water for 1 minute. Cool in ice bath. Reserve.

To Serve: Sear venison to medium-rare and slice into medallions. Reheat fava beans and asparagus. On each plate, place venison medallions, spice-glazed sweet potato, asparagus and fava beans. Drizzle with sauce. Garnish with fresh cilantro.

dessert/*serves 4*

Cherry Soup with Fromage Blanc

SOUP

1 cinnamon stick
3 star anise, crushed
5 cloves
3 allspice berries, crushed
2½ cups sweet red or white cherries, pitted
3 cups Pinot Noir or red Burgundy wine
¼ cup sugar
2 tablespoons lemon juice
4 tablespoons fromage blanc (for garnish)
mint leaves, julienned (for garnish)
cheesecloth

In a small piece of cheesecloth, bundle cinnamon stick, star anise and cloves. Set aside half of the cherries. Place the remaining cherries in a large saucepan with cheesecloth bundle and remaining ingredients. Bring to a boil. Lower heat and simmer for 2 minutes. Remove from heat, steep for 5 minutes, and discard cheesecloth bundle. Puree cooked cherry soup and strain back into saucepan through another cheesecloth. Add reserved cherries to saucepan with soup. Bring to a boil, then lower heat and simmer, covered, for 5 to 7 minutes.

To Serve: Transfer soup to bowls and garnish with fromage blanc and mint julienne. (Fresh ricotta may be substituted for fromage blanc if desired. Mix 4 tablespoons of ricotta with 2 tablespoons of lemon zest and 1 tablespoon of sugar.)

DECORATING

The New York Scene

Design:
Larry Gaines and Don Patt
Potts by Patt of San Diego

Bring the cool shade of summer indoors by setting the mood with an overlay of fresh foliage for this chic table setting. Simplicity is key, with understated accents of silver and cream that further enhance the natural beauty of the lemon leaf tablecloth demonstrated below.

- 1½ yards burlap cut into a square (large enough to cover table)
- 10 bunches of lemon or any sturdy leaf
- Craft or quick-drying glue
- Waxed paper
- Blocks or heavy books to serve as weights

First, place a cover over tabletop for protection—waxed paper or an old sheet will do. To prepare the base cloth, cut burlap in a square large enough to fit your table. Drape burlap over table and begin gluing individual leaves around the outer edge of table so that the pointed end of leaf overhangs edge.

Continue gluing leaves around circumference in a spiral pattern, making sure leaves overlap to create a shingled or "artichoke" effect. As you continue, place blocks or weights on top of leaves until glue sets. Cover entire surface until all burlap is covered. Accent tabletop with votives.

DOUGLAS RODRIGUEZ

Patria

New York, New York

"My mission is to teach New Yorkers about Latin American cuisine, to change their misconceptions about it," says executive chef and owner Douglas Rodriguez of Patria. "When most people think about Latin American food, they think of Mexico and Brazil, and they think that it has to be hot and fiery. What they don't know is that Latin American food may not be very fiery, but it's certainly well spiced."

Born in New York to Cuban parents, Rodriguez has had a fascination with food since his childhood. In his early teens he landed his first job in the kitchen in Miami. Rodriguez studied at Johnson and Wales Culinary University, graduating in 1985. After school he returned to South Florida to work at the Four Ambassadors, the Fontainebleau and the Sonesta Beach hotels. In 1989, Rodriguez opened the critically acclaimed Yuca Restaurant, with its innovative Nuevo Latino cuisine, and set the Miami restaurant scene on fire.

In 1994, Rodriguez opened Patria in New York City, and the critics are still raving. He has been nominated twice for "Rising Star Chef," in 1991 and 1993, by the James Beard Foundation, and was named "Chef of the Year, Miami" by the Chefs of America in 1991.

LOBSTER CEVICHE
with Hearts of Palm

SHREDDED TWICE-COOKED LAMB
over Boniato Purée with Black Bean Broth

CHICKEN ESCABECHE
with Fufu and Plantain Chips

PUTERIA DE MARISCOS

PEACH TRES LECHES

STARBUCKS SUMATRA COFFEE

appetizer/serves four

Lobster Ceviche with Hearts of Palm

LOBSTER MARINADE

- ½ cup freshly squeezed orange juice
- ½ cup freshly squeezed lime juice
- 3 tablespoons Dijon mustard
- 2 tablespoons dry English mustard
- 1 tablespoon mustard seeds
- 1 tablespoon horseradish
- 1 tablespoon chopped white onion
- ½ cup lobster stock
- 1 stalk of celery, diced

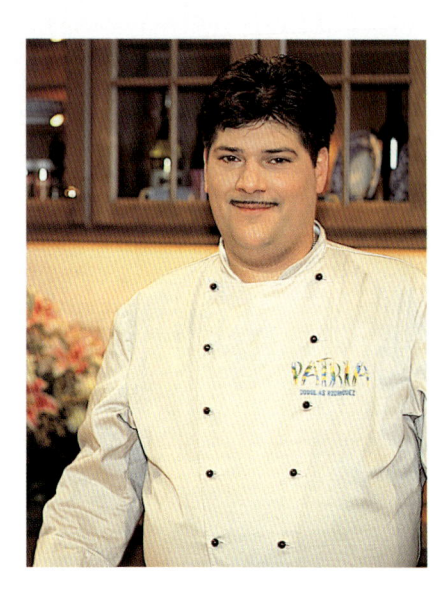

Lobster Ceviche with Hearts of Palm

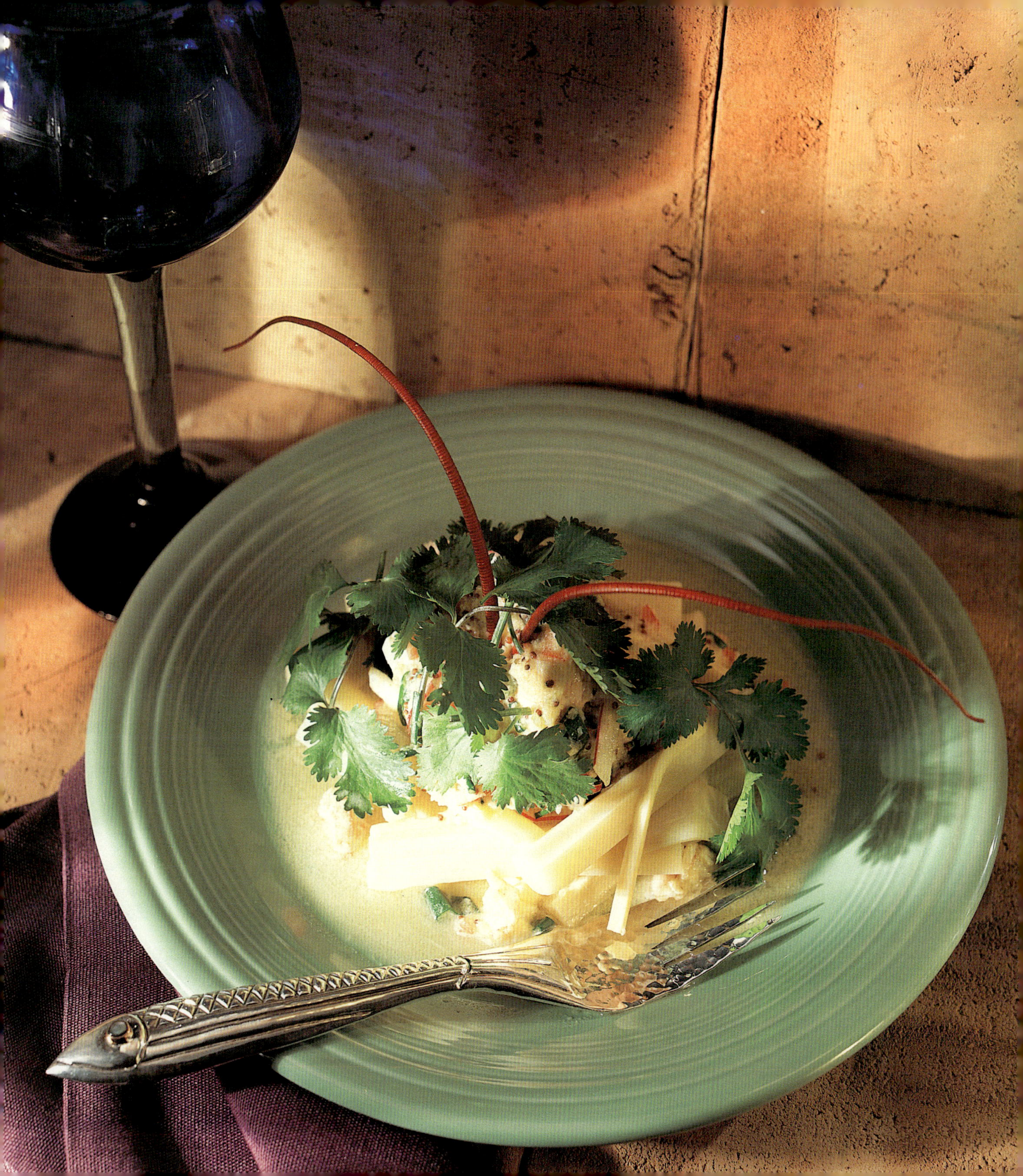

AMERICA'S HOTTEST NEW CHEFS

Starbucks Coffees Selected for America's Rising Star Chefs

Lively Impressions—Bright, Mild and Welcoming

House Blend
Our most popular coffee, bright and well-rounded.

Viennese Blend
Great with dessert—lively, with a smoky finish.

Costa Rica Tres Rios
Fragrant and tangy, with morning's brightness.

Ethiopia Sidamo
From coffee's birthplace... sweet and floral.

Rich Traditions—Deep, Complex and Satisfying

Caffè Verona® (80/20 Blend)
Rich and creamy, accented by a subtle sweetness.

Guatemala Antigua
Complex and elegant... with hints of cocoa and spice.

Colombia Nariño Supremo
Exclusively ours, full-bodied with walnutty flavor.

New Guinea Peaberry
Smooth and harmonious, an undiscovered treasure.

Kenya
Bright, rich and sweet, with hints of black currant.

Italian Roast
Darker than espresso—sweet and spirited.

Bold Expressions—Diverse, Distinctive and Intriguing

Sumatra
An enticing favorite... syrupy, deep and earthy.

Ethiopia Harrar
Wild and untamed, with berry-like flavor.

Combine juices, mustards, mustard seeds, horseradish, white onion, lobster stock and celery in a blender and blend well. Reserve.

CEVICHE

4	1½- to 2-pound Maine lobsters (about 4 to 4½ pounds cooked meat)
1	large yellow tomato, diced
1	small red onion, halved, then julienned
¼	cup cilantro leaves
¼	cup sliced scallions
¼	cup chopped chives
1	pound fresh hearts of palm

In a large mixing bowl, combine lobster, tomato, red onion, cilantro, scallions, chives and marinade. Toss and reserve. Steam hearts of palm for about 2 minutes, then chill in an ice-water bath.

To Serve: Lay some chilled hearts of palm decoratively on each plate. Place a scoop of lobster ceviche in center.

entrée / serves six

Shredded Twice-Cooked Lamb over Boniato Puree with Black Bean Broth

MARINADE

3	bay leaves
½	cup white vinegar
½	cup chopped white onion
¼	cup chopped cilantro
2	tablespoons chopped fresh thyme
2	tablespoons chopped fresh oregano
8	cloves garlic
2	tablespoons kosher salt
	black pepper (to taste)
1	tablespoon cumin seed
1	quart water

Put all ingredients except water in a food processor or blender. With the motor running, slowly add water to make a puree.

LAMB

- 1   3- to 4-pound boneless leg of lamb, trimmed of excess fat
- olive oil
- 3   tablespoons chopped fresh mint
- 1   small red onion, julienned
- 3   cloves garlic, thinly sliced
- 4   limes, juiced

Preheat oven to 325 degrees. Place leg of lamb in a non-aluminum pan large enough to hold both meat and marinade. Add marinade. Cover pan. Place pan in oven and cook for about 3 hours, or until very tender and almost falling apart. Remove from oven and let cool slightly. Using two forks, shred lamb. This preparation can be done in advance, and shredded lamb refrigerated. (Remainder of ingredients are used just before serving.)

BONIATO PUREE

- 2   pounds boniatos (pale sweet potatoes), peeled and diced

Chicken Escabeche with Fufu and Plantain Chips

4 cups milk, plus extra as needed
2 cups water

Place boniato, milk and water in a large pot. Bring to a boil and simmer for about 1 hour, or until fork-tender (like a potato). Drain. Mash boniato, adding enough milk to keep it moist. This can be made in advance and reheated in the microwave.

BLACK BEAN BROTH

1 pound dry black beans
2 bay leaves
1 teaspoon cumin
1 teaspoon minced fresh oregano
1 quart water
6 red bell peppers
2 white onions
20 garlic cloves

Place the beans, bay leaves, cumin, oregano and water in a large pot and simmer for 2 hours. Put peppers, onions and garlic through a juice extractor. Add juices to beans and cook an additional 30 minutes. Strain out beans and return broth to pot to reduce for another 20 minutes. This can be made in advance and refrigerated or frozen.

MINT MOJO

1 cup mint leaves
3 cloves garlic
3 tablespoons mint jelly
2 tablespoons red wine vinegar
3 tablespoons olive oil
salt and pepper

Place all ingredients, including salt and pepper to taste, in a blender and puree.

To Serve: Heat some olive oil in a large skillet. Add shredded lamb, red onion, chopped mint, sliced garlic and lime juice (juice last). Toss until crispy. Assemble a scoop of lamb on top of boniato puree and ladle some black bean broth over. Add a few dots of mint mojo.

entrée / *serves six*

Chicken Escabeche with Fufu and Plantain Chips

CHICKEN

6 chicken breasts
3 tablespoons olive oil
salt and pepper

Season chicken with salt and pepper. Heat oil in a skillet and sear chicken over medium-high heat for about 5 minutes per side, until nicely browned. Set aside.

ESCABECHE SAUCE

1 cup olive oil
1 cup julienned red onion
1 cup diced red bell pepper
1 cup diced yellow bell pepper
1 cup diced green bell pepper
3 tablespoons capers, rinsed
½ cup chopped black olives
2 medium ripe tomatoes, diced
¾ cup sherry vinegar
2 tablespoons tomato paste
½ cup ketchup
1 teaspoon chopped garlic
1 teaspoon chili powder
1 tablespoon salt

Place oil, onion, bell peppers, capers, olives and tomato in a large glass dish. Add chicken and mix together. Put vinegar, tomato paste, ketchup, garlic, chili powder and salt in a blender and puree. Add puree to chicken mixture and mix well. Cover dish tightly with foil and plastic wrap. Refrigerate overnight.

FUFU

6 slices bacon, diced
1 small onion, diced

3 ripe plantains, peeled and cut into large chunks

To peel plantains, cut ends off and make three lengthwise slashes through skin. Place in a sink filled with warm water for about 10 minutes. Peel will then remove easily.

In a sauté pan, cook bacon over medium heat for about 5 minutes. Add onion and continue to cook until bacon is crispy. Remove from heat and let cool. Meanwhile, bring a pot of water to boil and add plantains. Reduce heat and let simmer about 15 minutes or until soft. Drain plantains, then transfer to a bowl and mash with a potato masher. Fold in bacon and onion mixture. Keep warm.

PLANTAIN CHIPS

- 4 cups canola oil
- 2 green plantains, peeled and cut lengthwise into 1/8-inch-thick slices
- salt
- garlic powder

Heat oil to 350 degrees. Add plantains a batch at a time so that oil does not cool down. Cook 4 minutes per batch, or until golden brown. Remove to paper towels. Sprinkle with salt and garlic powder.

To Serve: Bring chicken escabeche to room temperature. Serve on plates with fufu and plantain chips.

entrée/*serves six*

Puteria de Mariscos

PLANTAIN "BASKETS"

- 2 large green plantains, peeled
- 1 3-ounce ladle
- 1 4-ounce ladle
- oil (for deep frying)

Cut plantains into thin round slices. Line 4-ounce ladle with slices. Spray bottom of 3-ounce ladle with no-stick spray and place inside other ladle. Lower plantain slices between ladles into oil for about 3 minutes, or until crunchy. Carefully remove from oil. Make six baskets and reserve. (A basket maker works better than the ladles and can be found in Asian grocery stores or kitchen supply stores.)

FRICASSEE DE MARISCOS

- 2 cups fish stock
- 2 cups white wine
- 2 tablespoons lime juice
- 1/2 cup diced onion
- 2 tablespoons ground garlic
- 3 ounces capers
- 3 tablespoons olive oil
- 1/2 pound shrimp, diced
- 1/2 pound grouper, diced
- 1/2 pound scallops, diced
- 1/2 pound calamari, diced
- 1 bunch fresh parsley, chopped
- butter
- salt and pepper

In a saucepan, combine fish stock, white wine and lime juice with onion, garlic and capers. Reduce by two-thirds and reserve.

Heat olive oil in a large sauté pan. Add shrimp, grouper and scallops and sauté about 2 minutes. Be careful not to overcook. Add reduced stock and reduce slightly more. Add calamari and parsley, and cook an additional minute or so. Finish with a little butter, and salt and pepper to taste.

GARNISH

- 1/2 red onion, thinly sliced
- 1/4 cup Niçoise olives
- 1 avocado, sliced
- 1/2 cup sour cream

To Serve: Spoon seafood fricassee into plantain baskets and place baskets on plates. Garnish plates with sliced red onion, olives, slices of avocado and sour cream.

dessert/*serves six*
Peach Tres Leches

CAKE

- 1 cup soft flour
- 1 teaspoon baking powder
- 5 eggs, at room temperature
- 1 cup sugar
- ¼ cup water
- 1¼ cups condensed milk
- 1¼ cups evaporated milk
- 1½ cups heavy cream
- ½ cup peach schnapps or other peach-flavored liqueur (amount may be adjusted as desired)
- pinch of salt

Preheat oven to 400 degrees. Lightly grease a 13-by-9-inch baking pan. Sift flour, baking powder and salt together and set aside. Place eggs in bowl of an electric mixer. Add sugar and start mixing on high. Add water all at once, and continue beating until mixture is fluffy and pale yellow. Pour in all of the flour mixture at once, and blend thoroughly and quickly in order to prevent eggs from losing volume. Pour into pan and tap firmly once or twice on a counter to remove air bubbles. Place in oven immediately and bake for 10 minutes, or until a toothpick comes out clean. Remove cake and let cool. Poke holes in top the cake with toothpick.

Blend milks, cream and schnapps with a wire whip and pour over cake. Refrigerate. (Any milk mixture left over makes a great milkshake with some ice cream and fresh peaches!)

MERINGUE

- 3 egg whites, at room temperature
- ⅓ cup white sugar
- ⅛ teaspoon vanilla
- ¾ cup powdered sugar

Warm the bowl and beaters of an electric mixer with hot water, then dry. Beat egg whites with sugar and vanilla until stiff. Working quickly by hand, blend in powdered sugar thoroughly. Place meringue mixture in a pastry tube or plastic sandwich bag with a hole cut in a bottom corner. Pipe out strips of meringue onto a sheet pan. Place in a 250-degree oven for about 1 hour, or until dry. This can be done a day in advance and the meringues stored in an airtight container.

POACHED PEACH GARNISH

- 6 peaches, peeled and halved
- 1 quart water
- 2 cups sugar
- 1 star anise
- 2 whole cloves
- 1 vanilla bean
- 1 cinnamon stick

Place all ingredients in a large pot and stir to dissolve sugar. Bring to a boil, then reduce heat and simmer until peaches are slightly soft (about 10 minutes, depending on ripeness of peaches). Remove peaches from poaching liquid and cool. Slice for plate decoration.

WHIPPED CREAM

- 1 cup heavy cream
- ¼ cup sugar
- ¼ teaspoon vanilla

In a well-chilled bowl with chilled beaters, beat cream with vanilla and sugar until firm. (Sugar can be omitted if desired.)

To Serve: Put one slice of cake in center of each plate. Decorate edge of plate with peach slices. Place a generous dab of whipped cream on cake. Top with more peach slices and meringue.

A Latin Fiesta

Design:
Bruce Stodola, ASID
Interior Design
Dos Cabezas, Scottsdale

The spirit and vitality of Latin American folk art enlivens the senses and awakens the palate for a sumptuous and spicy meal. A kaleidoscope of color and pattern enhances the festive atmosphere. There are no rules here, so use your imagination and create your own vision with the following suggestions:

Place wooden figures or sculpture on your table as a focal point.

For an alternative centerpiece and added drama, fill one or two large, open-mouthed, clear vases with water and immerse either flowers or fruit inside. Water magnifies and intensifies the objects. Long-stemmed flowers such as roses or tulips work best and can be sculpted along the inner curve of the vase. Fruit can be cut in half with the inside pressed against the glass to show off the pattern. Limes combined with cranberries look beautiful, for example.

Peruse craft shows or street fairs for unusual dishes or objects. Paint some of your own greenware and have it fired at a local craft shop.

Double-wrap two different colored napkins to create color when the perfect shade is not available.

Use a bolo tie or fun old jewelry as an alternative to a standard napkin ring, or wrap a strand or two of beads around a napkin and tie off in a loop.

Placemats can be made from an unexpected source at a local hardware store. Buy a large piece of screen in either brass or silver and cut it into a rectangle or circle for each placemat. Place a piece of glass cut in either shape over screen for each place setting.

If dining outdoors, throw down a mat or rug to keep dirt away and create space. Create your own mat by painting a piece of canvas or drop cloth with acrylic paints. Cut a stencil pattern from a potato or paint the backs of leaves and press down on cloth for a natural design.

DECORATING

115

INDEX

Italicized entries are the names of plates as they appear in the chefs' menus.

A

Ahi tuna tartare with fennel, caraway toast and green olive tapénade, 100–103
Aioli, red pepper–almond, with flash-fried squid, 12–13
Almond–red pepper aioli, with flash-fried squid, 12–13
Apricots and ginger baked in puff pastry with almonds, 62
Artichoke frittata, with grilled beef tenderloin, 81
Artichoke salad of summer tomatoes and spring beans, 24–27
Artichoke sauce, for oven-fresh red snapper, 74
Arugula and tomato salad, with pan-roasted chicken, 29
Asparagus sauce, for wide ribbon pasta (tagliatelle), 72–73
Avocado vinaigrette, for salmon salad, 7

B

Bacon, molasses and porcini vinaigrette, for pork tenderloin, 22
Balsamic vinegar glaze, for roast saddle of rabbit in savoy cabbage with Yukon Gold potato confit, 62
Balsamic vinegar sauce, for sautéed lamb chops, 73–74
Barley, carrot-infused, "risotto" of, with lobster, 56–58
Barley (pearl) "risotto" with braised fennel bulb, 35
Barley (pearl), savory, with a quartet of beef and a Riesling mustard sauce, 44–46
Basil-infused extra-virgin olive oil, 36–37
Basmati rice, with Thai curried swordfish, 89
Bass (striped), grilled farm-raised, in minestrone broth with braised Belgian endive, potato cake, soy beans and Parmesan cheese tuilles, 58–60
Bean (black) broth, for shredded twice-cooked lamb, 112
Bean (rice) ragout, with grilled escolar, 42–43
Beans (spring), in artichoke salad, 24–27

Beef, a quartet of, with savory pearl barley and a Riesling mustard sauce, 44–46
Beef tenderloin, grilled, with artichoke frittata, curried fried potato sticks and marrow, 81–82
  in a quartet of beef, 45
Beet juices, with roast saddle of rabbit in savoy cabbage, 62
Belgian endive, braised, with grilled farm-raised striped bass, 59
Bibb and watercress salad with hot mustard, toasted walnut bread and blue goat cheese, 92–94
Biscuits, with Frogmore stew, 67
Black bean broth, for shredded twice-cooked lamb, 112
Blackberry cobbler, 68
Blinis, potato, with citrus-marinated Atlantic salmon and garden greens, 34
Blueberry cake, with summer berries and farm cream, 98
Blueberry polenta cake, with corn crème brûlée, 90
Bolognese sauce, for grilled squab breast with foie gras, artichokes and wilted arugula, 53–54
Boniato (sweet potato) puree, with shredded twice-cooked lamb, 111–112
Braised lamb shanks and Portobello mushroom with slivered celery root and roasted garlic, 43–44
Brandy cream, for jumbo lump crabmeat, 86
Bread (croissant) pudding, chocolate banana, 8
Broccoli, in pastina "risotto," 21–22
Broth, black bean, for shredded twice-cooked lamb, 112
  garlic herb, for roasted-hazelnut-and-herb-crusted lamb with five-grain risotto, 80
  minestrone, with grilled farm-raised striped bass, 59
Brown sugar cream, for triple chocolate espresso cannoli, 82
Burnt-sugar cream, for warm bittersweet chocolate truffle cake, 38

C

Cake, blueberry polenta, with corn crème brûlée, 90

  New England blueberry, with summer berries and farm cream, 98
  peach *tres leches*, 114
  warm bittersweet chocolate truffle, with burnt-sugar cream, 38
Cakes, warm financier, with seasonal berries, 29
Cannoli, triple chocolate espresso, 82
Caramel-espresso sauce, for chocolate waffle and coffee ice cream, 16
Caraway toast, with ahi tuna tartare, 102
Cauliflower-potato puree, with sautéed lamb chops glazed in balsamic vinegar, 73
Celery root gratin, with slow-roasted duck, 15
Celery root, slivered, with braised lamb shanks and Portobello mushroom, 44
Ceviche, lobster, with hearts of palm, 108–110
Cherry soup with fromage blanc, 106
Chicken escabeche with fufu and plantain chips, 112–113
Chicken, lemon (roasted), with Moroccan olives, pine nuts, toasted garlic and couscous, 104–105
  pan-roasted, with oven-dried tomato and arugula salad, 29
  real pan-fried, 67–68
Chocolate banana croissant bread pudding, 8
Chocolate (bittersweet) truffle cake, warm, with burnt-sugar cream, 38
Chocolate tart, warm, with coffee nougatine sauce, 46
Chocolate (triple) espresso cannoli, 82
Chocolate waffle with coffee ice cream and espresso-caramel sauce, 16
Cilantro-citrus vinaigrette, for lobster cocktail, 78
Citrus vinaigrette, for garden greens, 34–35
  for vegetable slaw with Thai curried swordfish, 89
Citrus-cilantro vinaigrette, for lobster cocktail, 78
Citrus-marinated Atlantic salmon with potato blinis and garden greens, 32–35
Clam sauce, for Parmesan-coated monkfish, 88
Cobbler, fresh blackberry, 68
Coconut-lemongrass sauce, for Thai curried swordfish, 89–90

Coffee, about:
    blending, 58
    brewing fundamentals, 66
    brewing with a coffee press, 12
    coffeehouses, 20
    cooking with coffee, 42
    espresso, 86
    flavored syrups with coffee, 26
    matching with wine and foods, 94
    "A Passion for Coffee," 4
    regions, 50
    roasting, 34
    serving—away from the table, 72
    spiced coffee, 26
    Starbucks coffees, 110
    tasting terminology, 78
    tea or coffee, 102
Coffee ice cream, with chocolate waffle and espresso-caramel sauce, 16
Coffee nougatine sauce, for warm chocolate tart, 46
Colcannon-style mashed potatoes, with wood-grilled double-cut pork chops, 96
Compote, kumquat, 46
    tomato, with tian of Parmigiano and grilled vegetables, 52
Confit, potato, with roast saddle of rabbit in savoy cabbage, 62
Confit tomatoes, with mesquite-grilled tiger prawns, 48–50
Cookies, white cornmeal, 98
Copperwell sauce, for pasta and Chinese vegetables with grilled yellowfin tuna, 78–79
Coriander-crusted venison with spice-glazed sweet potato, 105–106
Corn crème brûlée with blueberry polenta cake, 90
Corn salsa, with salmon salad, 6
Corn whipped potatoes, with salmon and carrot nage, 20–21
Cornbread (for cornbread pudding), 14
Cornbread pudding, with pit-roasted salmon, 13–14
Cornish hens, oven-roasted, with spring leeks and Red Bliss potatoes, 37–38
Cornmeal (white) cookies, 98
Couscous, with lemon chicken, 105
Crab and fingerling potato salad, warm, with horseradish, crème fraîche and baby red oak lettuce, 40–42

Crabmeat, jumbo lump, with potato pancakes, mango and baby greens, 84–86
Cranberry-persimmon glaze, for wood-grilled quail, 96
Cream, brandy, for jumbo lump crabmeat, 86
    brown sugar, for triple chocolate espresso cannoli, 82
    burnt-sugar, for warm bittersweet chocolate truffle cake, 38
    espresso, for triple chocolate espresso cannoli, 82
    farm, for New England blueberry cake with summer berries, 98
Crème anglaise, for chocolate banana croissant bread pudding, 8
Crème brûlée, corn, with blueberry polenta cake, 90
Crispy red snapper with eggplant agrodolce, 104
Croutons, garlic, for saffron fish soup, 7
    for Tuscan mussel soup with white beans, 70
    walnut bread, for Bibb and watercress salad, 92–94
Curried fried potato sticks, with grilled beef tenderloin, 81

D

Decorating
    "A Bountiful Harvest," 99
    "A Casual Outdoor Affair," 39
    "A Colorful Poolside Oasis," 23
    "An Evening of Intrigue," 47
    "A Latin Fiesta," 115
    "A Middle Eastern Romance," 75
    "The New York Scene," 107
    "An Old West Picnic," 63
    "Old World Romantic Setting," 30-31
    "A 'Paradise Found' Tabletop," 9
    "A Personal Touch," 55
    "A Relaxed Luncheon Among Friends," 17
    "A Southern Marketplace Table," 69
    "A Table of Eclectic Crafts," 83
    "A Tropical Rendezvous," 91
Dressing, for Bibb and watercress salad, 94
Duck, slow-roasted, with green olives, fresh tomatoes and celery root gratin, 14–16

E

Eggplant *agrodolce*, with red snapper, 104
Eggplant caviar, with medallion of lamb with green and black Provençal olives and basil-infused extra-virgin olive oil, 36
Eggplant (roasted) and mozzarella, with tian of Parmigiano and grilled vegetables, 52
Escabeche sauce, for chicken, 112
Escolar, grilled, with rice beans, smoked garlic cloves, wild sage and a purple mustard sauce, 42–43
Espresso cream, for triple chocolate espresso cannoli, 82
Espresso-caramel sauce, for chocolate waffle and coffee ice cream, 16

F

Farm cream, for New England blueberry cake with summer berries, 98
Fennel, baby, with roast saddle of rabbit in savoy cabbage, 62
Fennel bulb, braised, with pearl barley "risotto," 35
    grilled, with mesquite-grilled tiger prawns, 50
Fennel, with ahi tuna tartare, 102
Financier cakes, warm, with seasonal berries, 29
Fish soup, saffron, with garlic croutons and rouille, 7–8
Fish, tandoori baked, 87–88
Flash-fried squid with red pepper–almond aioli and horseradish gremolata, 10–13
Fresh blackberry cobbler, 68
Fricassee, seafood (*puteria de mariscos*), 113
Fried chicken, 67–68
Frittata, artichoke, with grilled beef tenderloin, 81
Frogmore stew with biscuits, 66–67
Fruit salad, fresh, garnish for triple chocolate espresso cannoli, 82
Fufu, with chicken escabeche, 112–113

G

Garam masala, for tandoori baked whole fish, 87
Garlic herb broth, for roasted-hazelnut-and-herb-crusted lamb with five-grain risotto, 80

INDEX

Garlic (roasted) mashed potatoes, with lobster cocktail, 77
Garlic, roasted, with braised lamb shanks and Portobello mushroom, 44
Ginger and apricots baked in puff pastry with almonds, 62
Glaze, balsamic vinegar, for roast saddle of rabbit in savoy cabbage with Yukon Gold potato confit, 62
    Merlot wine, for hot smoked veal soufflé, 60
    persimmon-cranberry, for wood-grilled quail, 96
    tandoori, for fish, 87
Gratin, celery root, with slow-roasted duck, 15
Green onion sauce, for grilled Georgia mountain trout, 66
Greens, baby, with mango vinaigrette, 86
Greens, garden, with citrus vinaigrette, 35
Gremolata, for Parmesan-coated monkfish, 88–89
    horseradish, for squid, 13
Grilled beef tenderloin with artichoke frittata, curried fried potato sticks and marrow, 81–82
Grilled escolar with rice beans, smoked garlic cloves, wild sage and a purple mustard sauce, 42–43
Grilled farm-raised striped bass in minestrone broth with braised Belgian endive, potato cake, soybeans and Parmesan cheese tuilles, 58–60
Grilled Georgia mountain trout with green onion sauce, 64–66
Grilled squab breast with foie gras and artichokes, wilted arugula and sherry vinegar Bolognese sauce, 53–54
Grilled yellowfin tuna with pasta and Chinese vegetables in Copperwell sauce, 78–79

H

Herb crust, for roasted lamb, 80
Herb-crusted prawns with warm mushroom and potato salad, 4–6
Herb garlic broth, for roasted-hazelnut-and-herb-crusted lamb with five-grain risotto, 80
Horseradish gremolata, for squid, 13

Hot smoked veal soufflé with Merlot wine glaze, Italian parsley juice, grilled shiitake mushrooms and vegetable slaw, 60–61

I

Ice cream, coffee, with chocolate waffle and espresso-caramel sauce, 16
    mascarpone-mint, with fresh figs and vanilla-lemon syrup, 54

J

Jumbo lump crabmeat with potato pancakes, mango and baby greens, 84–86

K

Kumquat compote, 46

L

Lamb chops, sautéed, glazed in balsamic vinegar, 73–74
Lamb, medallion of, with green and black Provençal olives, eggplant caviar and basil-infused extra-virgin olive oil, 36–37
Lamb, mesquite-grilled, with tapénade and grilled Provençal vegetables, 53
Lamb, roasted-hazelnut-and-herb-crusted, with five-grain risotto, 79–81
Lamb shanks and Portobello mushroom, braised, with slivered celery root and roasted garlic, 43–44
Lamb, shredded twice-cooked, over boniato puree with black bean broth, 110–112
Leek-mushroom sauce, for oven-roasted Cornish hens, 37–38
Leeks, with oven-roasted Cornish hens and Red Bliss potatoes, 37
Lemon chicken with Moroccan olives, pine nuts, toasted garlic and couscous, 104–105
Lemongrass-coconut sauce, for Thai curried swordfish, 89–90
Lemon-vanilla syrup, for mascarpone-mint ice cream, 54
Lentil (red) and quinoa pilaf, with wood-grilled quail, 96–97
Lobster ceviche with hearts of palm, 108–110
Lobster cocktail with roasted garlic mashed potatoes, 76–78
Lobster, with "risotto" of carrot-infused barley, 56–58

M

Mango vinaigrette, 86
Marinade, for beef, 81
    for lamb, 110–111
    for lobster in lobster ceviche, 108–110
Mascarpone-mint ice cream, fresh figs and vanilla-lemon syrup, 54
Medallion of lamb with green and black Provençal olives, eggplant caviar and basil-infused extra-virgin olive oil, 36–37
Merlot wine glaze, for hot smoked veal soufflé, 60
Mesquite-grilled lamb with tapénade and grilled Provençal vegetables, 53
Mesquite-grilled tiger prawns with pesto, cannellini beans, grilled radicchio, fennel and confit tomatoes, 48–51
Minestrone broth, with grilled farm-raised striped bass, 59
Mint mojo, garnish for shredded twice-cooked lamb, 112
Mint-mascarpone ice cream, 54
Molasses, bacon and porcini vinaigrette, for pork tenderloin, 22
Monkfish, Parmesan-coated, 88–89
Moroccan (green) olive and pine nut sauce, for lemon chicken, 105
Mozzarella and roasted eggplant, with tian of Parmigiano and grilled vegetables, 52
Mozzarella and tomatoes, spiedini of (skewered), 18–20
Mushroom and potato salad, warm, with herb-crusted prawns, 6
Mushroom (Portobello) and lamb shanks, braised, with slivered celery root and roasted garlic, 43–44
Mushroom-leek sauce, for oven-roasted Cornish hens, 37–38
Mushrooms, in tart with potatoes and spinach, 27–28
Mushrooms (shiitake), grilled, with hot smoked veal soufflé, 61
Mussel soup, Tuscan, with white beans, 70–72
Mustard (purple) sauce, for grilled escolar with rice beans, 43
Mustard Riesling sauce, for a quartet of beef with savory pearl barley, 45

INDEX

N

New England blueberry cake and stone-ground white cornmeal cookies with summer berries and farm cream, 98
Niçoise sauce, for salmon with olive oil mashed potatoes, 28

O

Olive (green) tapénade, for ahi tuna tartare, 102–103
Olive (Moroccan green) and pine nut sauce, for lemon chicken, 105
Olive oil, basil-infused, 36–37
Olive oil mashed potatoes, with salmon and sauce Niçoise, 28
Olive sauce, for medallion of lamb, 36
Olive-tomato sauce, for slow-roasted duck, 15
Onion (green) sauce, for grilled Georgia mountain trout, 66
Onion sauce, for wood-grilled double-cut pork chops, 95–96
Oven-fresh red snapper with artichokes and fresh oregano, 74
Oven-roasted Cornish hens with spring leeks and Red Bliss potatoes, 37–38
Oxtail, in a quartet of beef, 45

P

Pan-roasted chicken with oven-dried tomato and arugula salad, 29
Pancakes, potato, with jumbo lump crabmeat, 84–86
Parfait of "crazy raspberries," 22
Parmesan cheese tuilles (for garnish), 60
Parmesan-coated monkfish, 88–89
Parmigiano (cheese) and grilled vegetables, tian of, with tomato compote, fresh buffalo mozzarella and roasted eggplant with pesto, 51–53
Parsley juice, with hot smoked veal soufflé, 60–61
Pasta (linguini) and Chinese vegetables in Copperwell sauce, with grilled yellowfin tuna, 79
Pasta, wide ribbon (tagliatelle), with asparagus and basil, 72–73
Pastina "risotto" with roasted peppers and broccoli, 21–22

Pastrami, veal, 97–98
Pastry (puff), apricots and ginger baked in, with almonds, 62
Peach tres leches, 114
Pearl barley "risotto" with braised fennel bulb, 35
Pearl barley, savory, with a quartet of beef and a Riesling mustard sauce, 44–46
Pepper(s), red, see Red pepper(s)
Persimmon-cranberry glaze, for wood-grilled quail, 96
Pesto sauce, for mesquite-grilled tiger prawns, 50–51
for tian of Parmigiano and grilled vegetables, 52
Phyllo tart of mushrooms, potatoes and spinach with mushroom jus, 27–28
Pilaf, quinoa and red lentil, with wood-grilled quail, 96–97
Pine nut and Moroccan (green) olive sauce, for lemon chicken, 105
Pit-roasted salmon with shiitake relish, cornbread pudding and fried basil, 13–14
Plantain baskets, for seafood fricassee (puteria de mariscos), 113
Plantain chips, with chicken escabeche, 113 garnish for Thai curried swordfish, 89
Polenta cake, blueberry, with corn crème brûlée, 90
Porcini, molasses and bacon vinaigrette, for pork tenderloin, 22
Pork chops, wood-grilled double-cut, with colcannon-style mashed potatoes, 94–96
Pork tenderloin with molasses, bacon and porcini vinaigrette, 22
Portobello mushroom and lamb shanks, braised, with slivered celery root and roasted garlic, 43–44
Potato and mushroom salad, warm, with herb-crusted prawns, 6
Potato (fingerling) and crab salad, warm, with horseradish, crème fraîche and baby red oak lettuce, 40–42
Potato blinis, with citrus-marinated Atlantic salmon and garden greens, 34
Potato cake, with grilled farm-raised striped bass, 59–60
Potato confit, with roast saddle of rabbit in savoy cabbage, 62

Potato pancakes, with jumbo lump crabmeat, 84–86
Potato sticks, curried fried, with grilled beef tenderloin, 81
Potato-cauliflower puree, with sautéed lamb chops glazed in balsamic vinegar, 73
Potatoes, boiled fingerling, with crispy red snapper, 104
colcannon-style mashed, with wood-grilled double-cut pork chops, 96
corn whipped, with salmon and carrot nage, 20–21
olive oil mashed, with salmon and sauce Niçoise, 28
roasted garlic mashed, with lobster cocktail, 77
in tart with mushrooms and spinach, 27–28
Prawn sauce, for herb-crusted prawns with warm mushroom and potato salad, 6
Prawns, herb-crusted, with warm mushroom and potato salad, 4–6
Prawns (tiger), mesquite-grilled, with pesto, cannellini beans, grilled radicchio, fennel and confit tomatoes, 48–51
Pudding, chocolate banana croissant bread, 8
cornbread, with pit-roasted salmon, 13–14
Puree, boniato (sweet potato), with shredded twice-cooked lamb, 111–112
potato-cauliflower, with sautéed lamb chops glazed in balsamic vinegar, 73
Puteria de mariscos, 113

Q

Quail, wood-grilled, with spiced cranberry and persimmon glaze and a pilaf of quinoa and red lentils, 96–97
A quartet of beef with savory pearl barley and a Riesling mustard sauce, 44–46
Quinoa and red lentil pilaf, with wood-grilled quail, 96–97

R

Rabbit, roast saddle of, in savoy cabbage, Yukon Gold potato confit, balsamic vinegar glaze, baby fennel and beet juices, 61–62

INDEX

Radicchio, grilled, with mesquite-grilled tiger prawns, 50
Raspberries, "crazy," parfait, 22
Real pan-fried chicken, 67–68
Red lentil and quinoa pilaf, with wood-grilled quail, 96–97
Red pepper juice, for crispy red snapper with eggplant *agrodolce,* 104
Red pepper–almond aioli, with flash-fried squid, 12–13
Red peppers, roasted, in pastina "risotto," 21–22
Red snapper, crispy, with eggplant *agrodolce,* 104
  oven-fresh, with artichokes and fresh oregano, 74
Red wine (Pinot Noir) sauce, for coriander-crusted venison, 105
Red wine sauce with marrow, wild mushrooms and prosciutto, for grilled beef tenderloin, 81–82
Relish, shiitake, 14
Rice (Basmati), with Thai curried swordfish, 89
Rice bean ragout, with grilled escolar, 42–43
Riesling mustard sauce, for a quartet of beef and savory pearl barley, 45
Risotto, five-grain, with roasted-hazelnut-and-herb-crusted lamb, 80–81
"Risotto" of carrot-infused barley with lobster, 56–58
"Risotto," pastina, with roasted peppers and broccoli, 21–22
"Risotto," pearl barley, with braised fennel bulb, 35
Risotto with porcini mushrooms, with Parmesan-coated monkfish, 88
Roast saddle of rabbit in savoy cabbage, Yukon Gold potato confit, balsamic vinegar glaze, baby fennel and beet juices, 61–62
Roasted-hazelnut-and-herb-crusted lamb with five-grain risotto, 79–81
Rouille, for saffron fish soup, 7

S

Saffron fish soup with garlic croutons and rouille, 7–8
Sage vinaigrette, for watermelon salad with feta and sumac, 4

Salad, artichoke, with summer tomatoes and spring beans, 24–27
  Bibb and watercress, with hot mustard, toasted walnut bread and blue goat cheese, 92–94
  crab and fingerling potato, warm, with horseradish, crème fraîche and baby red oak lettuce, 40–42
  mushroom and potato, warm, with herb-crusted prawns, 6
  salmon, with avocado vinaigrette and corn salsa, 6–7
  tomato and arugula, with pan-roasted chicken, 29
  watermelon, with feta, sumac and sage vinaigrette, 2–4
Salmon salad with avocado vinaigrette and corn salsa, 6–7
Salmon (Atlantic), citrus-marinated, with potato blinis and garden greens, 32–35
  pit-roasted, with shiitake relish, cornbread pudding and fried basil, 13–14
Salmon with corn whipped potatoes and carrot nage, 20–21
Salmon with olive oil mashed potatoes and sauce Niçoise, 28–29
Salsa, corn, with salmon salad, 6
Sauce, artichoke, for oven-fresh red snapper, 74
  asparagus, for wide ribbon pasta (tagliatelle), 72–73
  balsamic vinegar, for sautéed lamb chops, 73–74
  Bolognese, for grilled squab breast with foie gras, artichokes and wilted arugula, 53–54
  clam, for Parmesan-coated monkfish, 88
  coconut-lemongrass, for Thai curried swordfish, 89–90
  coffee nougatine, for warm chocolate tart, 46
  Copperwell, for pasta and Chinese vegetables with grilled yellowfin tuna, 78–79
  escabeche, for chicken, 112
  espresso-caramel, for chocolate waffle and coffee ice cream, 16
  green onion, for grilled Georgia mountain trout, 66

  leek-mushroom, for oven-roasted Cornish hens, 37–38
  Moroccan (green) olive and pine nut, for lemon chicken, 105
  mustard (purple), for grilled escolar with rice beans, 43
  Niçoise, for salmon with olive oil mashed potatoes, 28
  olive, for medallion of lamb, 36
  olive-tomato, for slow-roasted duck, 15
  onion, for wood-grilled double-cut pork chops, 95–96
  pesto, for mesquite-grilled tiger prawns, 50–51
  pesto, for tian of Parmigiano and grilled vegetables, 52
  prawn, for herb-crusted prawns with warm mushroom and potato salad, 6
  quick, basis for olive sauce for lamb, 36
  red wine (Pinot Noir), for coriander-crusted venison, 105
  red wine, with marrow, wild mushrooms and prosciutto, for grilled beef tenderloin, 81–82
  Riesling mustard, for a quartet of beef with savory pearl barley, 45
Sautéed lamb chops glazed in balsamic vinegar, 73–74
Savoy cabbage, with roast saddle of rabbit, 61–62
Seafood fricassee *(puteria de mariscos),* 113
Shallot rings, with salmon salad, 6–7
Sherry vinaigrette, 52
Shiitake mushrooms, grilled, with hot smoked veal soufflé, 61
Shiitake relish, with pit-roasted salmon, 14
Shredded twice-cooked lamb over boniato puree with black bean broth, 110–112
Slow-roasted duck with green olives, fresh tomatoes and celery root gratin, 14–16
Snapper, red, see Red snapper
Soufflé, hot smoked veal, 60–61
Soup, cherry (dessert), 106
  saffron fish, with garlic croutons and rouille, 7–8
  Tuscan mussel, with white beans, 70–72
Spiedini of mozzarella and two tomatoes with basil oil, 18–20

INDEX

Spinach, in tart with mushrooms and potatoes, 27–28
Squab breast, grilled, with foie gras and artichokes, wilted arugula and sherry vinegar Bolognese sauce, 53–54
Squid, flash-fried, with red pepper–almond aioli and horseradish gremolata, 10–13
Stew, Frogmore, with biscuits, 66–67
Strawberries with zabaione, 74
Striped bass, grilled farm-raised, in minestrone broth with braised Belgian endive, potato cake, soybeans and Parmesan cheese tuilles, 58–60
Sweet potato, spice-glazed, with coriander-crusted venison, 106
Sweetbreads, in a quartet of beef, 44–45
Swordfish, Thai curried, 89–90
Syrup, vanilla-lemon, for mascarpone-mint ice cream, 54

T

Tandoori baked whole fish, 87–88
Tapénade, green olive, for ahi tuna tartare, 102–103
Tart, phyllo, of mushrooms, potatoes and spinach with mushroom *jus*, 27–28
Tart, warm chocolate, with coffee nougatine sauce, 46
Thai curried swordfish, 89–90
Tian of Parmigiano and grilled vegetables with tomato compote, fresh buffalo mozzarella and roasted eggplant with pesto, 51–53
Tiger prawns, mesquite-grilled, with pesto, cannellini beans, grilled radicchio, fennel and confit tomatoes, 48–51
Toast, caraway, with ahi tuna tartare, 102
Tomato and arugula salad, with pan-roasted chicken, 29
Tomato compote, with tian of Parmigiano and grilled vegetables, 52
Tomatoes and mozzarella, spiedini of (skewered), 18–20
Tomatoes, confit, with mesquite-grilled tiger prawns, 48–50
Tomatoes, in artichoke salad, 24–27
Tomato-olive sauce, for slow-roasted duck, 15
Triple chocolate espresso cannoli, 82

Trout, grilled Georgia mountain, with green onion sauce, 64–66
Tuilles, Parmesan cheese (for garnish), 60
Tuna (ahi) tartare, with fennel, caraway toast and green olive tapénade, 100–103
Tuna (yellowfin), grilled, with pasta and Chinese vegetables in Copperwell sauce, 78–79
Tuscan mussel soup with white beans, 70–72

V

Vanilla-lemon syrup, for mascarpone-mint ice cream, 54
Veal feet, in a quartet of beef, 45
Veal pastrami, 97–98
Veal soufflé, hot smoked, with Merlot wine glaze, Italian parsley juice, grilled shiitake mushrooms and vegetable slaw, 60–61
Vegetable slaw, with hot smoked veal soufflé, 61
  with Thai curried swordfish, 89
Vegetables (Chinese) and pasta in Copperwell sauce, with grilled yellowfin tuna, 79
Vegetables (grilled) and Parmigiano (cheese), tian of, with tomato compote, fresh buffalo mozzarella and roasted eggplant with pesto, 51–53
Vegetables, grilled, with mesquite-grilled tiger prawns, 50
Vegetables (Provençal), grilled, with mesquite-grilled lamb, 53
Venison, coriander-crusted, with spice-glazed sweet potato, 105–106
Vinaigrette, avocado, for salmon salad, 7
  cilantro-citrus, for lobster cocktail, 78
  citrus, for garden greens, 34–35
  citrus, for vegetable slaw with Thai curried swordfish, 89
  mango, 86
  molasses, bacon and porcini, for pork tenderloin, 22
  sage, for watermelon salad with feta and sumac, 4
  sherry, 52
Vinegar, balsamic, *see* Balsamic vinegar

W

Waffle, chocolate, with coffee ice cream and espresso-caramel sauce, 16
Warm bittersweet chocolate truffle cake with burnt-sugar cream, 38
Warm chocolate tart with coffee nougatine sauce, 46
Warm crab and fingerling potato salad with horseradish, crème fraîche and baby red oak lettuce, 40–42
Warm financier cakes with seasonal berries, 29
Watercress and Bibb salad with hot mustard, toasted walnut bread and blue goat cheese, 92–94
Watermelon salad with feta, sumac and sage vinaigrette, 2–4
Wide ribbon pasta (tagliatelle) with asparagus and basil, 72–73
Wine (Merlot) glaze, for hot smoked veal soufflé, 60
Wine (red) sauce, for coriander-crusted venison, 105
Wine (red) sauce, with marrow, wild mushrooms and prosciutto, for grilled beef tenderloin, 81–82
Wood-grilled double-cut pork chops with colcannon-style mashed potatoes, 94–96
Wood-grilled quail with spiced cranberry and persimmon glaze and a pilaf of quinoa and red lentils, 96–97

Y

Yellowfin tuna, grilled, with pasta and Chinese vegetables in Copperwell sauce, 78–79

Z

Zabaione, with strawberries, 74
Zucchini flowers, deep-fried (for garnish), 58

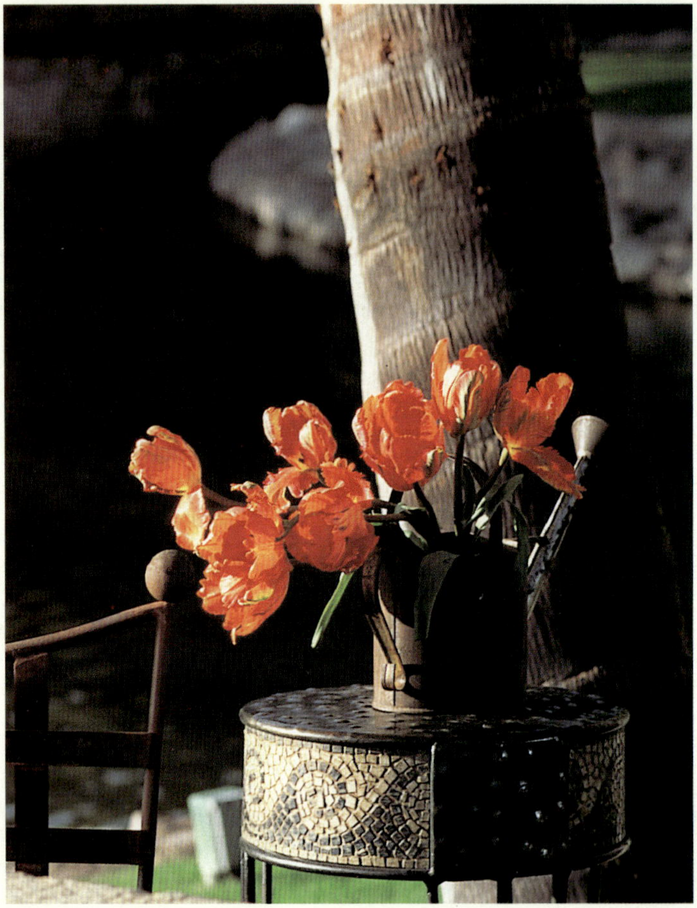